The
Happiness
System
for Women

The
Happiness
System
for Women

The Truth about Creating
a Happy and Fulfilling Life

A Step by Step Guide
by

ALEXANDRA WATSON

W Publishing

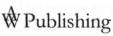
Publishing
HappinessAuthor@aol.com
www.AlexandraWatson.com

Cover by Tim Lochmueller

ISBN:0-9760088-0-7

CONTENTS

PART ONE
The Truth About Happiness

Stage Two: The Happiness Myths

Stage Three: Your Map To Happiness

Stage Four: Personal Power

PART TWO
The Heart Of Happiness

Stage Five: Make Way For Happiness

Stage Six: Creating True Happiness

Stage Seven: How To Live Happily Ever After

ACKNOWLEDGEMENTS

I am truly blessed and grateful because I have so many wonderful people in my life. So there are many I would like to thank for their support and encouragement. My first and biggest thanks go to my husband Matti. His staunch support, belief in my abilities, massive amounts of love and unwavering patience has helped me stay on course. I love you darling.

I would also like to thank my family and friends who have been wonderful in their feedback, ideas and sheer sweetness. Some friends have been so hands-on with such incredible stamina I could not have completed the book without them, so thank you ladies! Thanks also goes to my dog Pebbles. She faithfully sat by my side hour upon hour as I endeavored to complete this book. Bless you darling dog for being such a great companion.

Inspiration has come to me in many forms, but the actual life changing kind has come from Mark Victor Hansen, Robert Allen, Iyanla Vanzant, Napolean Hill, Don Miguel Ruiz, Dr Norman Vincent Peale, Gary Zukav, John Gray, Tony Robbins and Oprah to name but a few. Thanks go to them and to the other hundred or so mentors of mine.

Many thanks go to my clients who allowed me to use some of their stories within the book. I only hope that you learned as much from me as I did from you.

I also want to thank all the women I have ever had the fortune to meet at my seminars. You are all such phenomenal people and are the creators of our world's future. This book is for all of you with much love.

INTRODUCTION

YOUR GUIDE TO HAPPINESS

'Happiness is created not found.' **Alexandra Watson**

Congratulations! By having this book you have made the first step towards life-long happiness. You are about to learn what you were never taught at school, namely, how to be happy. You are in for an amazing education that may be one of the most important things you do for yourself and your family. This book is written as a system and contains all the information you need to create a truly happy and fulfilling life. All you have to do is read it and apply it.

When it comes to happiness, my philosophy is that we create it rather than find it. We create it from within. Happiness is not out there somewhere waiting for us to trip over it. We cultivate it from the inside. Happiness is a special gift we give ourselves and this system helps you do just that.

By applying these seven stages, you will discover how real happiness works and how little it has to do with birthright, luck, or winning the lottery. Happiness is no accident either. The people who are genuinely and superbly happy in life have made it so themselves. I have devised this powerful personal course to show you how you too can create happiness and keep it in your life forever.

This system is simple, non-academic, easy to follow and highly-effective. It can help anyone who is ready and willing to be exceptionally happy. My systematic approach towards creating happiness enables you to master each stage. It is a fusion of many effective philosophies, exercises and wisdom that lead you through a specific sequence of learning. You will find that each step continues on from its predecessor and at the same time builds a foundation for the next.

This book is for women because I wanted to create a system of happiness principles that could help people just like me. I wanted to help people with the same issues and circumstances as me. I know that sometimes life can seem hard and extremely stressful, but I have learned over the years that real happiness is possible and easier than you could ever imagine. That is why I created this guide to the *truth* about happiness. I want to share with you what I have learned both personally and professionally about creating a fulfilling life. If you study this book and become a student of happiness and its principles, you will learn the secrets in a fraction of the time it took me. You will learn to stop striving in life and simply start developing who you are.

I believe that women are phenomenal creatures. We are nurturing, compassionate, capable, intelligent, sweet and kind. We are employees, employers, daughters, sisters, aunties, nieces, grandmas, wives, moms, lovers and friends. We exist as if there are twenty seven hours in the day and are frequently stretched in several directions to the point of exhaustion. But this 'busy-ness' can sometimes only allows us to live a mediocre life instead of building ourselves a life masterpiece. The trouble is, not many of us believe that we can be really happy and so settle for mere sanity instead. More often than not, we just strive to survive. Which raises the questions; why do we set our standards so low? What are we afraid of? And why do we feel so undeserving?

Typically, we put others before ourselves and often feel enormous amounts of guilt if we want to take a break from it all. I believe we deserve more and so this book is for all women who think the time has come to make some improvements but don't know what to do or where to start.

We are never given detailed information about how to improve our lives so we have to go looking for it, or we simply struggle along day to day. I wanted to change all that and so put all the relevant information on how to be happy and fulfilled in one book and made it very easy to follow.

All the strategies that enable you to become more self-confident, self-loving, successful and of course, happy in your lifetime are right here in this book. To me it is a tragedy that society ignores this amazing information, most of which has been around for many years. It has just not been available in one place and accompanied by interactive life-coaching techniques until now. My book is an attempt to rectify society's omission and make what we *should* know readily available for everyone, even men!

When it comes to the truth about happiness, this book will be a re-assessment and a re-education of what you know to be true in life. It goes into depth about the happiness myths many of us *still* believe in. Also it discusses the programming or 'scripting' of society and the common perceptions we have of life that only serve to fail us. It's important for you to know the differences between the truth and a myth when it comes to happiness. This is because *real* happiness can only come from what is true, it simply cannot come from anywhere else. Yet many are occupied in their search for *false* happiness. We strive to get material things, great careers or the things we feel we *should* have. However, true happiness comes from your understanding and practice of how it is genuinely created. This book will provide what you need as far as the information and know-how is concerned, but it is up to you, dear reader, to put the work in. You reap what you sow and this is especially true when it comes to this system. The work involved is fun, inspiring and enlightening and you will discover great things about yourself and your world. After completing each stage you will not only be a little wiser, but more loving to yourself and others. This in turn, will instantly improve the quality of your life and the lives of those around you.

Treat this book as your insurance policy against unhappiness and pass on what you learn to others. The truth strategies and exercises contained within this book aim to help you connect with your inner-self so you can expand your world in a way that is right for you. Therefore, it is not directly related to any specific religion.

In my opinion, two things hold you back from being happy right now. The first is a lack of self-awareness or knowledge about your inner-self and the second is a lack of real commitment to yourself. Both can be built upon throughout this system. So I urge you to take the plunge and dive straight in. Absorb all the knowledge and opportunities for growth this book has to offer. I have endeavored to use as much information from other women as possible and again urge you to pass on what you learn to the women you treasure in your world.

About This Book

This system aims to provide you with all the tools you will ever need to have a happy and fulfilling life. It is divided into two parts and seven stages. Part One discusses the truth about happiness. We shall take a look at your personal programming and how it has affected your life so far.

Stage One helps you to define where you are right now in your life. You get to create your own personal definition of happiness and learn about your needs and the power behind your thoughts.

Stage Two exposes all the myths about happiness and how we have been fooled by them over the years. You will learn the meaning of authentic happiness as well as what you *don't* need to be happy. We take you through your emotional fears and phobias that have been limiting your happiness so far. Additionally, you will be taught which mindset is necessary for happiness and how to obtain it.

Stage Three covers the eight main elements of happiness. It tells you what they are, how they relate to you and how to make significant improvements in each area step by step.

Stage Four explains what personal power is and how to develop yours. You will learn about the fundamental elements of who you are, what makes you tick, what you want and how these can be used to create your happiness.

It also covers other powerful areas that affect your happiness like self-sabotage and your intentions.

Part Two is about the heart of happiness. Now that you have demolished what has been holding you back by completing Part One, you are now ready to know the secrets of creating real happiness. You will learn how to create it authentically and, therefore, for the rest of your life.

Stage Five is about preparing the way for an abundance of happiness. Get ready to tackle your belief system, how you talk as well as who and how you love.

Stage Six gets to the nuts and bolts of how to create happiness. It takes you through the importance of perspective, self control and your values.

Stage Seven, the final section of 'The Happiness System for Women,' teaches you how to be happy for the rest of your life. It is essential that what you have learned in this book never leaves you. So it not only teaches you how to build a truly happy life, but how you can take what you know to the next level. It's life mastery.

I cannot emphasize enough the importance of reviewing what you have worked on at the end of every stage. Not only will it give you an opportunity to clarify your understanding of what you have just learned, but also how to enhance it. Each Stage has a review section, these are essential reading.

At the end of this book, I share with you invaluable resources. I have included a list of self-development books as well as details of coaching organizations. This is not just another self-improvement book. My aim was to create a system that works developed from an anthology of some of the best minds that have ever lived. It will teach you the power of listening to yourself and questioning what you believe. Take time to listen to yourself. Listen to what your heart tells you, to what your soul says and to what your body is trying to communicate to you. This is the very essence of personal development.

THE TRUTH
Happiness Is For You Too!

I didn't use to be the truly happy person that I am today. Really, I didn't. I may have appeared to be, but on the inside I was struggling. My story mainly revolves around how my family moved a lot when I was young. The constant moving helped me become good at making friends, but I had to leave them behind when I moved again. I never felt settled or secure. Eventually my natural confidence began to fade the more towns I moved to and new schools I attended. By the time we did settle in one place my parents divorced and we moved once again.

When you live like this it is instinctive to either attach yourself to something or become a rebel. I did the latter. My rebellion was a mild one by anyone's standards but to my mother, who was bringing up three girls by herself, it was very upsetting. My angst was aimed at her, but in effect all I was doing was expressing my insecurity.

After graduating college I became a marketing and PR professional. It felt right at the time but little did I know back then I was living as I thought I *should* and not as I truly wanted. I worked my heart out in the wrong profession but life has a funny way of telling something is not quite right. In my case work began to become a real chore. However, I pushed on even though everyday meant less until I eventually came to a complete stop. I finally realized I was unhappy. I wanted a new vocation and I wanted to do something I loved. This decision meant making a substantial change in my life. It was agonizing because I was leaving an industry I knew well to start from scratch. Until now my career had been a big part of my identity and was all I knew, but I had an overwhelming sense that I had to become the person I was *meant* to be.

Changing one's life is never straight forward, but it is amazing. I felt the fear of letting go, of moving on and taking a leap of faith. The one thing I was beginning to understand was that in order to be happy I had to be true to myself. I had to do *something* with my life that honored my most important values. I still wanted to help people, but on a higher level. This is when I discovered the profession known as Life Coaching. I knew instantly that it was for me. I studied hard and qualified quickly. As well as coaching teams, executives and private individuals, my work rapidly developed towards writing articles, manuals, reports, creating the Women's Life Improvement Club (www.wliclub.com), and of course, writing this book. Go to the website above to get a free subscription to my monthly newsletter on happiness, fulfillment and life improvement for women.

I now have the best job in the world. I am able to help people to help themselves. It is unbelievably rewarding and I am so grateful to be able to do it. Coaching is one of today's fastest growing industries. Many people are finding that they are unfulfilled at work or at home, or simply want to get ahead in life and have discovered that coaching is a perfect aid to becoming unstuck and making huge leaps forward in life. The essence of coaching is in the unlocking of a person's potential to maximize their life. The focus is always on possibility rather than on past mistakes. Coaching helps a person overcome their worst enemy, their inner-critic. As coaches we believe that everyone can excel once they know how to dismantle self-limiting beliefs and self-doubt. Also, coaches help people create certain behavioral changes to propel them forward to create happier and richer lives. Now thousands upon thousands of people have a life coach. Everyone can benefit enormously from having a coach. Even coaches have a coach. All successful people have a coach and you should too. Through this book, I can be your coach. I will coach you through the changes and discoveries you are about to make. Use me and this book as your support system, mentor and cheerleader. I totally believe you can do anything you want to. Why? Because if I was able to then you can too!

The Price Of Not Trying

I cannot think of anything quite as terrible as having a fantastic opportunity pass you by because you let it. Being happy is not just a fantastic opportunity, it is your right. Let's face it, we *want* to be happy, we *need* to be happy. After all, what else is as important in life besides your health? Though when do we ever have the time in our hectic lives to do anything about being happy? And even if we do, how do we know that what we are doing is right?

I want to make a deal with you right now. Make a commitment to yourself. A real commitment that you will be open to experience all of what happiness has to offer you in your lifetime without feeling guilty. My part of the deal is to support you for as long as you need me. Do we have a deal?

The real price of not trying, or not making a commitment, is to decide to have a mediocre life. Some people may interpret mediocre as safe, familiar and stable. I see it as insecurity, frustration and tedium. Choosing 'safe' is opting for a life of limitations. I firmly believe that we owe it to ourselves and the rest of the world, to make a commitment to create happiness. Then we can give back to the world the gift of our true self.

The yearning we have deep down inside to reach our full potential is not a dream. We have been programmed to believe that dreams are just for dreamers and that change takes too much time and effort. We are comfortable with the philosophy of no pain, no gain however, I believe happiness is not a luxury but the reason that we exist. Some people ask why bother even trying? Why risk the life they have now? We often rely on things like work, eating, sex or shopping to feel alive, but it is happiness that creates our true riches, peace and power. Most of us are happy to go along with a level of status and reasonable material circumstances but this is merely comfort in conventionality.

Our ultimate duty is to our calling, our uniqueness and our insistence on being our self. When we start to become what we were meant to be, other people's approval is no longer needed, life is easier and so we create a new freedom.

Being successful in creating happiness is not so much fixing a major flaw, but is more to do with seeing to the small details of your everyday life. Can you imagine what our world would be like if we devoted as much time, effort and determination to studying happiness as we do creating wealth or planning a vacation? Why don't we spend the time when the rewards are so great? I can only put it down to a lack of faith in ourselves. Many of us choose a life of drifting in and out of happiness, powerless against perplexing attacks of unhappiness. If only more people would make this commitment to themselves, then their lives and our world would improve dramatically.

Assuming that you have decided to make a commitment to yourself, you have to prepare yourself for a re-education. This means taking a good hard look at what you already know and believe to be true and question its authenticity, origin and value.

The Truth About Your Life

'If you can't find the truth right where you are, where else do you think you will find it?' **Buddha**

Hands up if you tend to stick your head in the sand like an ostrich when it comes to tackling anything emotionally difficult or painful? We are sometimes afraid of, and therefore hide from, the truth. But if we want to be happy we need to change our approach. Truth is one of the most important things in life. It is something to value highly, not spurn. Knowing the truth about our lives is a pre-requisite for creating happiness.

Life without truth is stressful but it is amazing how many of us choose to live a lie rather than embrace it. The pain of living a lie is worse than facing the truth. No matter how much we like to hide from the truth, we will never fully escape it. Inevitably, it will haunt us like a ghost. It will be a constant reminder of what needs to be healed or changed until we take action. Perhaps you are experiencing a 'truth ghost' in your life right now?

Facing the truth may not always be easy, but the truth is always simple. With this in mind, the exercises in this book are going to be very different from anything you have done before. This is because they will help you uncover your truth and stretch and challenge you like all good learning experiences. There may be moments when you feel like giving up. But don't. Don't deny yourself the many rewards life has to offer. Perhaps you think that you don't have the time. By taking a little extra time for yourself to complete this book, you will be helping those you love just as much as you will be helping yourself. As you grow into a happier person, everyone around you will benefit too.

You are about to learn a new system, one that you can personalize to work well for you. Get ready to peel back some emotional layers to become more self-aware. You will get to know yourself thoroughly as you learn what's true for you and what's not. It is a fact that no one can be truly happy without really knowing themselves. Knowledge is the path to growth, so enjoy this part of your journey. It will be amazing and totally worth your effort.

How To Use This Book

I have written this book as a professional coach so that it acts as a coach for you. All the exercises are created in a similar way to how I conduct coaching sessions. This system will help you learn quickly and from deep within yourself. Like a coach, the book helps you to use your inner-resources to unveil your own powerful answers and true direction in life.

The dynamics of learning this way ensures that you make the right improvements for you. As you work through this book you will begin to tune into your inner-self and see real miracles start to happen.

This book is written in stages for you to create happiness in a structured and progressive manner. Each stage has powerful interactive exercises or visualizations. Try these out to see the stimulating influence they have on your subconscious mind.

Set a quiet time to complete each stage. Take your time and work through the book to the best of your ability. There is a great deal of information to absorb, so take it one step at a time. The stages have been placed in a specific order. Attempting them in any other way may not be as effective. Similarly, skim-reading this book will not be helpful at all. Skipping stages or not doing the stage reviews is not using the book as the complete system it is intended to be. For the best results, start at the first stage and work your way through carefully and thoroughly.

Approach each stage with a view to learning something new and dynamic. This will give you the energy and enthusiasm to absorb and process all the information. It is quite possible to complete this book within a week, but I urge you to give yourself as much time as you need. It will work well for you no matter what your background or current situation is. It will be effective if you are single, married, employed, self-employed or a homemaker.

Extra Tip

Before you start Part One, I highly recommend that you start a journal. It will be an invaluable companion for you on your journey. Journals remind you of your thoughts, fears, hopes, dreams and big learning moments. You can refer back to your journal whenever you want to or use it just to make notes. What's really amazing is that once you have completed this book, your journal will show you just how far you have come.

What To Expect On Your Journey

When you finish this book you will have given yourself a great gift - the gift of happiness. Even if you do not manage to complete the book you will still learn some powerful lessons. Remember, what you will be reading is wisdom that has been developed over hundreds of years. Each stage touches upon personal issues like your beliefs, values, frustrations and personal boundaries, giving you a chance to think about them probably for the first time in your life. Give yourself the gift of patience and take your time to think deeply and thoroughly about each area of the book. Also, you will get the best results from being as honest as possible. Remember, truth is the key! No exercise is too long or too difficult, but they may be challenging. You are about to launch yourself out of the nest so you can learn to fly. The more you put into it, the more you will get out of it and I promise it will be an amazing experience.

Review each stage, taking the time for reflection and assessment of your progress. And as a last piece of advice, if you get stuck on a particular subject leave it for a day and then come back to it and try again. But do go back.

What To Expect From Yourself & Others

You are going to love this experience and what it does for your life. You'll get excited about the 'aha' moments and the answers you gather about life. You will grow beyond your wildest expectations and astound friends and family with your enhanced wisdom and renewed zest for life. Expect that you will experience emotional ups and downs. You may feel confused or unwilling to make any changes. This is all part of the growing process and the resistance you feel is from the transformation involved with improving your life. Simply acknowledge how you feel and carry on doing your best. Also, there may be things you don't quite get, or questions you cannot answer straight away. This is where your commitment and determination come in. Be strong and be kind to yourself.

Be patient with yourself too. This is one of the reasons why I strongly suggest you start a journal to accompany the exercises you do.

Expect to learn at your own pace and not anyone else's. Remember, this is *your* journey and *your* experience, so enjoy it. Expect other people to scoff at you. This is because they are in a different place on their own journey. Perhaps they feel vulnerable by your development. Fears like this can bring out the worst in people, so be prepared for friends and family to question your particular direction and path that you find yourself on right now. If this does happen, all you have to do is acknowledge their feelings and try not to take what they say personally. Whatever happens, don't let them stop you moving ahead.

One more important point is that you may be familiar with some of the topics we touch upon in this book. We shall be covering a wide variety of self-development topics including goal-setting and clutter clearing (good old Feng Shui!). You may already know the information intellectually, which is great. What you may not yet know, however, is the information *emotionally*. There is a big difference between intellectual and emotional intelligence. Knowing something intellectually does not mean that you actually use that information, it just means you know *of* it. Knowing something emotionally happens when you have experienced it personally. This is why some people remain skeptical about self-improvement. They perhaps have been to a self-help or motivational seminar or have read a few books, but have remained the same person in the same situation. What they missed was the opportunity to learn the information in an emotional way.

Take this opportunity to learn emotionally by working through the exercises as best as you can. Write your answers with as much detail as possible for maximum impact and development. Be open-minded and willing to look at things in a different way so you can learn a great deal.

Know that your self-development is a life-long journey and that this book is a crucial step forward. This system has been designed to be valid for your *whole* life. Come back and revisit any stage or exercise whenever you need to. Finally, expect that your life will change for the better. Be open and honest on your journey, expect that you will create an abundance of happiness and know that you deserve it.

Are you ready to start? Great, let's go!

PART ONE

THE TRUTH ABOUT HAPPINESS

This book is all about happiness, so let me spell it out for you:

Honesty

Abundance

Purpose

Persistence

Intuition

Nurturing

Enlightenment

Self-awareness

Self-love

Introduction

Part One explores the truth about happiness, examining what it is and what it is not. We have been programmed for most of our lives to believe that happiness is either this or that. I invite you now to take the opportunity to find out what happiness is really all about. Getting clear about happiness is the first stage. It has been my experience that when asked, many people don't really know what happiness means to them. We shall look at why this is and how you can crack the code when it comes to defining what happiness is for you.

Happiness seems to be a subject that attracts many myths regarding its substance and occurrence. That being the case, people can make up some outstanding reasons why they believe they are not happy. This section takes you on an in-depth journey through why we do this and at what level you are perhaps a little guilty of myth creation.

During the course of this book, I will be asking you many questions with the intention of getting you to think deeply and with guidance from your inner-self. One such question asks you to calculate where you are right now emotionally in certain areas of your life. In coaching, it is imperative for the client to determine exactly where they are in terms of their life, dreams and expectations. If you know where you are, which I shall call A, then you have a better chance of determining where you want to go, which is B. Then you can work out how far A is from B and how you are going to get from A to B.

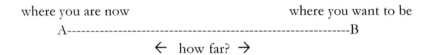

Part One ends with a very powerful section on personal power. This phrase is being widely used in many of today's self-improvement books and so I will take you through what this means and how it relates to you.

I am sure you will be delighted with the insights you learn about yourself throughout this section and indeed the whole book. Take a tip from me; pay particular attention to the truth when you answer the questions in the following exercises. This is because you will soon discover that the truth about creating happiness is the truth about you.

Stage One

What Is Happiness?

'Wherever you are is always the right place. There is never a need to fix anything, to hitch up the bootstraps of the soul and start at some higher place. Start right where you are.' **Julia Cameron**

In this first stage you will learn the following:

- How to identify real happiness
- How to identify what happiness is to you
- How to identify what happiness is not
- How to discover what's holding you back
- How your thoughts can change your life

Here we shall address your beliefs about happiness. This is because you need to know exactly what happiness is to you. As I mentioned earlier, there are myths about happiness and there is genuine happiness, so we shall look at where your beliefs lie. Our beliefs are deeply embedded within our psyche so we need to excavate any misguided ones to make a fresh start.

You may have questions about where you are heading in life, but for the moment you need to focus on letting go of your past. If we let them, our pasts can have an extraordinary hold over us and our future. If your past was not so hot, then don't let it have a future. Understand that your past does not really matter. Your future does not have to be the same. Neither does your future have to be the same as your mum's, dad's, sister's or brother's. For example; just because your parents never made it big don't assume that you won't. Similarly, just because your mother is a lawyer, it doesn't mean that you have to be one too. Your genes or family traditions have nothing to do with your happiness or success. Don't let them negatively influence you or stop you reaching for what you want.

Throughout this book, you will be learning and growing. As your self-limiting beliefs and bad habits evaporate, you will start to become the person you were *meant* to be. Acknowledge the fact that this book is your opportunity to make a fresh start. You have absolutely no limits on where you can end up. Take a moment. I want you to start leaving your past behind you right now. Take a deep cleansing breath and exhale slowly. Relax your body as you let the air out. Do this several times while thinking; 'my past is not my future and I am living now as I was meant to.'

This is a declaration or affirmation to use as often as you like. Phrases like this are very helpful in dissolving any chaotic or negative thoughts to give you clarity and peace of mind instantly. You are creating your present and your future in one small, positive sentence. If you repeat this affirmation often enough it will penetrate into your subconscious. Then, magically, it starts to find ways to make it happen. Affirmations are useful in many situations. When you create your own make them positive and in the present tense.

Meditating is also a great way to create a peaceful mind. There are many excellent books on the subject, some of which I have included in the resources section at that back of this book. You can use affirmations and meditation at any time to encourage and develop peace of mind if ever you feel anxious or overwhelmed. Try them both for yourself and see how they make you feel.

Getting Permission

Before we go any further, I just want to ask you a question: Have you got permission to be happy? It may seem a strange question to ask, but it is a fact that many people feel they need permission to be happy or to succeed at anything in life. Needing permission is rarely a conscious thought, so let's make sure that this need is not lurking in the back of your mind somewhere. If it is we need to get rid of it otherwise it will sabotage your progress. The need for permission is something we learn in childhood. Getting permission from our parents or teachers is something we learn early on in life and as adults we often still seek our parent's approval. Part of becoming an adult is accepting the freedom and responsibility that comes with making our own choices and decisions. However, having our parents' permission or approval can still be of great value to us. The beauty of being aware of this is that you can now give *yourself* the permission to be happy. Say the following out loud: 'I hereby give myself permission to be truly happy.'

This simple act is your ticket to accepting that what you are doing is ok. It strengthens your objective of leaving the past behind you to forge ahead. Sometimes, just giving yourself permission can help you with life's little obstructions. For example, give yourself permission to say yes or no in any situation, or give yourself permission just to be yourself.

How To Identify Real Happiness

Now it's time for us to put happiness under the microscope. You are going to study it closely because you need to know what it means to you on a very personal level. You need to know which aspects of happiness you identify with and therefore want in life. This might not be as simple as you first imagined. You want to be happy, but what does that mean to you?

You have to know what happiness is for you before you can have it. Otherwise you spend many fruitless and frustrating years searching for it in all the wrong places. It's like going clothes shopping with plenty of money to spend but with only a vague idea of what you want to buy. Now this may sound like fun, but you can spend all day visiting every single store. You try on many different items, but nothing seems right, so you give up and go home. Or worse, because you really want to get something, you end up panic-buying. It is only when you get home do you admit that what you bought really doesn't suit you at all. This is a metaphor for how we sometimes approach happiness. We may be ready and willing, but do we actually know what we are looking for? And how many times in our lives has our eagerness to be happy made us buy into the wrong thing? Being vague about happiness equates to a waste of your time and money, so you need to get clear.

Many women have romantic ideas about happiness. We often believe that one day someone will come and save us from all this madness. Worse still, some believe that true happiness doesn't exist at all and is just an ideal. And there are some who believe happiness is one of life's mysteries, a rare and fragile prize. Finally, some have what I call a 'lottery mentality.' They treat happiness as something to be won. They live their lives waiting and hoping it will be their turn soon, only if they are lucky enough.

The moral of all this is that many people leave their happiness to chance or to someone else, instead of creating it for themselves. The truth is, happiness can only be created by ourselves. Ask yourself the following:

- What are my true feelings about happiness?
- Do I think becoming truly happy is possible?

Make a decision about your possibility of success in being able to create a happy and fulfilling life before you start.

Choose to have an easy experience and be resolute about it. Forget about how things have been in the past. Take the opportunity to arm yourself with a firm decision that you will be very happy and then go all out to prove yourself right. Making positive choices is vital to your happiness so start making them now. Choose to be successful at creating happiness no matter what.

How To Define What Happiness Is To You

This exercise will help you uncover how you feel and what you know about being happy. The process involves both your imagination and your memory. You are going to recreate an image of happiness in your mind that will enable you to build a picture of your future. Answer these questions as truthfully and as completely as you can. Find a quiet spot, take out your journal and take as much time as you need.

1. What Makes Me Happy?

Make a list of all the things that *make* you happy in life. These can be big or small. Include as many of them as you can. Making a simple list of what makes you happy gives you the opportunity to really think about your feelings. Just doing this exercise can make you feel happy.

2. What Does Happiness Look Like?

Next I want you to write down what happiness *looks* like to you. Write down whatever scenes or objects come to mind. Use your imagination and memory to create a snapshot. Make sure your vision comes from you and is not one that has been adopted from elsewhere. Use as much detail as possible, have fun with it and let your imagination run free. Focusing on what happiness looks like allows your subconscious mind to exercise its powers. The images you choose to depict happiness during this exercise are a direct pathway to your true desires.

3. How Do I Feel When I Am Happy?

Now think about how you *feel* when you are happy. Try to articulate your feelings as much as you can. Do you feel light, carefree, energized or do you feel calm and peaceful?

4. My Happiest Times So Far.

Next, write down a list of the happiest times in your life so far. I do hope it is a long list! This part is a lot of fun so enjoy it.

If you feel you have never truly been happy and therefore cannot answer some of the questions, think about your expectations of happiness. What do you *think* you will feel, hear or see?

A Quick Review:

Now you have a chance to really learn something about yourself by reviewing what you have written. Consider these review questions:

- How easy was it to answer these questions with your *own* ideas about happiness?
- Were you trying to answer the questions with adopted beliefs of what you *thought* it should be?
- Think about how you have defined happiness so far. Do you want to make any changes to it or add anything at all?

In short, think about how happiness looks, feels and sounds like to you. It is important for you to know *what* you feel when you are happy.

Picture This

Using your power of thought and imagination you can use visualization as a happiness technique. It is a simple yet effective tool that only requires you to relax and focus. Don't worry if your imagination takes a little time to warm up. Indeed, it may have been a while since you used it, so keep trying this exercise until you feel comfortable with the images that your mind creates.

Go back to question four when you were thinking about your happiest times. Pick one of them and close your eyes. In your mind's eye visualize that moment.

Once you have a clear image, start to enhance it. Imagine yourself there in the picture and then answer these questions with as much detail as possible:

- Where are you?

- What are you doing?

- What are you thinking?

- Who are you with?

- What can you see?

- What can you hear?

- How do you feel?

Simply doing this exercise can make you feel good. You are bringing back to life a time when you were happy. This is your picture of happiness and one that you can go back to whenever you like. Go back to it often. Develop it carefully and thoroughly by adding color, sound and detail because the stronger the image you have, the stronger your feelings of happiness will be.

The power of visualization is huge. It is a great tool to have. You can create whatever mood or feeling you wish simply by imagining it. Try it for yourself. Go back and imagine different times in your life and recreate them in your mind. See how the images you have affect how you feel. Play with it and use it to your advantage. Visualization techniques like this are often used by people to create a certain state of mind to help them both personally and professionally. How else can it help you?

How To Identify What Happiness Is Not

Now you have a good idea about what happiness is for you, this next section looks at what happiness is not. Again, you have to think about what is true or not for *you*. Take your journal and write down all the things that you know *don't* make you happy. Think of the things you have chased in life that have left you feeling disappointed. Fill in the blanks for each one:

I thought...............would make me happy because.........

I now know that it doesn't because...............................

    Now that you have examples of all the things that appeared to be happiness but were not, go through each one and then answer the following:

My main disappointment was......................................

Because it made me feel...

I now know happiness is never disguised as......................

or...................................... or.............................

    This exercise exposes what happiness is not. It is important to make a note for each example you have so you can see clearly why you were mistaken and what you subsequently learned. These were your happiness myths and we will be covering more in Stage Two.

How To Discover What's Holding You Back

Believe it or not, we all have needs. They vary from person to person and in their intensity and importance. Having certain needs can be rather a tricky business, because depending on their nature, your whole life can be dictated by them. Therefore, the quality of life you are enjoying right now is directly related to your very own set of needs.

Now let's be clear about the meaning of the word 'needs.' In this particular context I am talking about your emotional needs as opposed to your physical everyday ones. Your emotional needs can drive you to do many things as easily as they can stop you dead in your tracks. Obviously, you cannot be happy in life if you are not aware of what your needs are. The same is true if you ignore them. If your needs are not being met you may feel irritated, frustrated, resentful, deprived or even angry. For all of us, the key is to determine where our needs come from so we can have a better understanding of ourselves and conscious control over our actions. As we respond deeply to our needs we want to avoid a life of reacting irrationally to uncomfortable situations. Being aware of our needs will help us to master self-control.

Having needs is not altogether a bad thing. We just have to be aware of what they are because we unconsciously try to satisfy them. It is easier to identify what your needs are by thinking about the emotional areas of your life, like your relationships with loved ones for example. Our needs actually leave clues to their existence through curious little rituals or habits we may have. They can range from frequently falling out with your family or friends, to procrastination or overspending. As common as these may seem, they are all examples of behavior serving a need. You will be surprised at how many of our traits actually come from our natural compulsion to satisfy a need.

Exercise

Think through the following questions and answer them as honestly as possible. Start by copying the table below into your journal.

1. Take the first heading and write down what needs you think you have. Here are just some examples of needs out there: The need to...

be accepted	be acknowledged	be right	be needed
be in control	be loved	be cherished	be heard
be approved	be thanked	be seen	be liked

2. When you have done this, then answer the second, third and fourth questions in relation to each of the needs you have listed.

1 What are my needs?	2 What do I do to satisfy them?	3 When I do satisfy them, how do I feel?	4 If I don't satisfy them, how do I feel?

Need Example: *I have a need to be accepted. To satisfy this need I do and say things to fit in with others. When I have satisfied this need it leaves me feeling low and frustrated. If I don't satisfy the need then I feel anxious and nervous about what people think of me.*

This is an excellent exercise to really get in touch with your inner-self. Needs can hold you back, so take the time to expose and understand them so you can clear the way ahead. Try not to confuse your needs with desires. These are of course quite different as they don't limit you like needs can. Desires are internal hints as to what you want for yourself. We will be talking about desires later on in this book.

Be gentle with yourself during this exercise. We are talking about deep-set emotions, so don't be judgmental. Learn with compassion and with a view to deepening your understanding about yourself.

Insights & Explanations
Knowing your needs and how you satisfy them can throw light on why you sometimes behave the way you do. Ever wondered why you can't say no to some people? It usually boils down to a need to be liked. So if your behavior is unflattering in any way, or if you don't feel good about what you are doing, take a look at the need or needs you are serving. Sometimes just unveiling a need is enough to make it disappear for good. However, some may require more attention. This self-discovery process is about digging deep down inside to see exactly what needs you have.

The first step is to be very aware of what you are doing most of the time. This may sound impractical and in fact impossible, but try and stop just for one minute and ask yourself what you are doing and why. Creating a habit like this will help you become more conscious of your subconscious behavior. If the answers you get point towards being needy then you have the choice of whether to stop your reactive behavior or not. What you decide to do with this inner-knowledge is a testament to the connection you have with your true self. It's about doing what you feel is right. The sooner you get to know the needs you have, the sooner you create happiness. Your success both now and in the future comes from knowing and being more yourself.

Free Yourself

This next exercise may well help you do just that. Go through these questions and answer them as honestly as you can. Look at the needs you identified and write down what benefits they have for you, i.e. what do you get from having this need?

Next, write down when you think you adopted the need. There are certain times in our lives like upsetting or frustrating experiences, when needs are created. When did you first acquire yours?

Getting an insight into when you first adopted a need can put your behavior and feelings into perspective. Ultimately, it is vital that you take responsibility for your needs. Don't expect other people to know what they are or resolve them for you. The solutions have to come from within you, so always look to yourself for the answers first. Free yourself from your needs and do it with patience and kindness.

The 'Making Other People Happy' Trap

Women get into real emotional difficulties when we feel the need to make other people happy. I have heard many women say they make a certain someone happy. This is usually in their intimate relationships. Some even believe that they can save a person. The intention sounds extremely noble, but the truth of the matter is that no one can save, help or be a happiness solution for anyone else. It seems that women especially believe that by making other people happy they are making themselves happy. Only short term results are ever achieved this way because being happy is something we all have to do by ourselves first. Likewise, no person can make us happy. Someone may make us feel secure which we may confuse with happiness, but if that person leaves, then we become unhappy once more.

Be careful whose hands you leave your happiness in, no matter how much you love them. They can take happiness away from you at any time. No one can be responsible for your happiness except you. Similarly, trying to be responsible for someone else's is making promises that cannot be kept and sets a relationship up for failure. Many women know this on an intellectual level but still practice it emotionally. Relationships with others should be a bonus, not a salvation.

We have to *own* happiness ourselves before we can give it away. You cannot give away what you don't have. Don't be someone who spends many fruitless years trying to make someone else happy. It is impossible. So if you are doing this in a relationship stop right now! You are wasting your time and energy. Deep down you probably already know this. The key is to spend time making yourself happy first.

Real-Life Story

Georgina came to me frustrated with her life and wanted to do something about it. Her feelings had been building up over a long period of time and were starting to affect how she related to those around her. First she expressed how guilty she felt for being frustrated because she knew her life was better than most. After all, she had a great marriage and two wonderful kids.

Feelings of Guilt

Guilt is a useless emotion that helps no one. It stops us from learning or understanding what we need to. It is used widely in our society to feel bad about who we are, how we feel, what we do and how we do it. The truth is, when it comes to guilt we can choose to feel it or not. Either way, it doesn't stop us from doing things to feel guilty about. So it serves no purpose at all.

Having decided to acknowledge her feelings without feeling guilty, Georgina and I talked about what was causing her frustration. Behind the issue we discovered that she was actually anxious about her husband's health. She felt he was overweight and was worried that as he was fast approaching forty five, it may cause him some health problems. Georgina told me how often she had put him on a low-fat diet and had bought him new exercise equipment. But doing this for him had only worked for a while. Eventually he would give up the diet or the exercise which left Georgina feeling hurt. She felt he didn't love her enough to try harder. She wondered why he didn't do what she asked him to when it was the best for him. They argued about it but Georgina didn't want to risk their marriage so she backed down in the end. However, this did not stop her constantly feeling let down and frustrated by his behavior.

The Coach Approach
Georgina was attempting to control her husband's life. She believed that if he did what she said...or what she wanted him to do, he would be happy. As a wife she should be able to tell her husband what to do right? Wrong! No matter what relationship you have with another person you are not responsible for making them happy. It is up to them to make themselves happy.

Her husband was resisting her attempts at changing him by stopping the exercising and diet programs after a short period of time.

The Result
Georgina realized that even though her intentions were good, she had to let him decide what to do on his own terms. She confessed that it was hard not to make suggestions about how he should diet and exercise, but soon saw that he was getting on with it by himself. Georgina discovered that he wanted to lose weight, he just didn't want to be managed by anyone when he did so.

The Conclusion
People always have a reason behind their behavior. Their reason may seem strange to us, but it is their personal reason. It should always be up to the individual to change their behavior because they own both their reasons and their behavior.

It is a natural instinct to want to help those we love. Sometimes we can fall into the trap of trying to organize them because we know we are capable of doing so and it is a way of showing our love. We cannot fix, change or save anyone, even those we love dearly. So the best way to show our love is to simply listen to them and let them know we are there for them.

A Burning Yearning

Yearning for something is what most coaches call 'being in want.' It is similar to having needs. Ironically, your wants and needs will keep you from getting what you deserve, so it is important that you examine them closely. You have to go through the same process as you did with your needs to see how your wants affect your life.

When we yearn for something it's usually for what is comforting or familiar, like an ex-boyfriend for example. We know that getting back with him may not be the best thing for us, but we still have a yearning. It is an inner-battle. When we yearn, we are thinking without our emotional intelligence and the whole episode becomes a big distraction. The truth is, we are looking for a quick fix to feel better. We often get obsessed with feeling better fast instead of taking the time to heal the real issue behind the want. Healing an issue is often about understanding its origin and why it exists. Once you have acknowledged the issue, extract the negative beliefs. You will learn how to do this later on in the book.

This section offers you the opportunity to reveal your longings and their meaning. Think about them for a moment. Here are just some examples of the real issues that are perhaps behind them: If you are thinking about going back to an old relationship that didn't work before, then you are yearning intimacy or feelings of security. Similarly, if you are anxious about finding your next partner you are looking for others to make you feel complete - which is all about feelings of low self-worth. Most of the time we yearn for what we feel is missing in our life, but the real issue can be about something entirely different. Put your attention and energy into the real issues so you can heal them and move on.

Exercise

Copy the chart below in your journal and answer the questions in each heading as completely as possible:

What am I yearning for?	Why do I crave this?	How will it affect my life if I get it?

The Agony & The Ecstasy

By completing this exercise, you are becoming more aware of yourself and exposing the truth behind why real happiness has eluded you for so long. It can be an insightful experience because you are exposing a vulnerable side of yourself. The result of overcoming your yearnings is long-term joy. It is worth doing the inner-work now to reap the rewards for the rest of your life. The opportunity of going through self-awareness exercises like this is rare. Unless you have a personal life coach, where else would you have the chance? This is why it is essential to seize this time and make the most of it.

We all have wants and needs in life and can suffer because of them. So don't feel you are alone. What does make you special, however, is your commitment to yourself for coming this far in this book and believing that you deserve better. So acknowledge this fact about yourself. Take a look at what you have written about your wants and how they affect you on a daily basis. Once again, let me say all these exercises are here to help you, so always be kind but honest with yourself.

Go back to the chart. Take your answers from the column with the heading 'How will it affect my life if I get it?' See if any of what is written below is similar to your answers. Is there a certain person's name that fills in these blanks?

It will affect my life because....

.... will like me
.... will accept me
.... will respect me
.... will love me
.... will need me

Ask yourself whether you are looking for other people or the outside world to improve your life. The truth is if you can satisfy a yearning to be accepted, respected or loved from within yourself, you would no longer have any yearnings. As I keep saying, it is totally possible to create an abundance of happiness by yourself.

How Your Thoughts Can Change Your Life

'Thoughts are energy, and you can make your world or break your world by your thinking.' **Susan L Taylor**

Women are big thinkers. We live so much in our minds and process everything emotionally. We are wonderfully complex, but our emotional nature can sometimes be perceived as a weakness. This is because of the lack of understanding about how we tick.

For example, we may be perceived as hysterical when we are merely expressing our anger or fear. Or we may appear confused when we are just analyzing our feelings carefully. I believe our internal emotional connection is a great strength. I urge you to embrace who you are and never feel embarrassed or be apologetic about it, no matter how emotional you get. Our thoughts are a big part of who we are and how we experience life. More importantly, our thoughts carry messages to us from our inner-self.

Our minds are constantly thinking but we are not always conscious of it. We analyze, cogitate, contemplate and create continually. The problem is, most of us suffer from what I call 'stinking thinking.' Because our thoughts create our reality, if our thinking stinks, then so do our lives. Thoughts are extremely powerful. The quality of your thoughts directly affects the quality of your life. You are where you are today because of how you think.

We shall be talking about how we think in more depth at various stages throughout this book. For now though, since you have started to learn about monitoring what you do and why you do it, start checking your thoughts too. This means you have to start becoming more aware of what you are thinking each day. This of course takes practice.

This simple two-step exercise is a good way to help you get started:

1. Write your main thoughts down every single day at the end of each day, or whenever a particular thought stands out.

2. Then take a look at the *quality* of the thoughts you have noted. Are they negative in any way?

This exercise is amazing as you can immediately improve the quality of your thoughts and, therefore, your life.

Because we think at the speed of light, we rarely notice *how* we are thinking so this exercise gives you a chance to take mental snapshots of your thoughts. Once you have a good idea about the positive or negative status of your thoughts, you can start to make moves towards improving them. Remember, thoughts are very powerful. So learning how to harness this power is an exceptionally valuable tool.

The following is an example of a Thought Journal. It's exactly what I would like you to start from now on. I have added what I call *Coach Approach* comments that improve the quality of the writers initial thought. By doing this, you can see the difference between a negative approach and a more proactive or positive one. In this example, the writer recorded her main thought of the day. You may wish to record more. I have simply added my comments to them and you can do the same. First record your thoughts and then add a more positive replacement below them. Focus on what lies behind your thoughts. For example, if you have recorded your day's thoughts and they are concerning one incident or person, ask yourself what is really bothering you about the situation. Learning about the feelings behind your thoughts will put you in a position to resolve any painful or annoying issues you may have.

Thought Journal

Monday 6th
Main Thought Of The Day:

I have been thinking about my workload and wondered how I am ever going to get it all completed this week.

Coach Approach

Behind this thought is the feeling of being overwhelmed. If you feel that you have too much on your plate, it will lead to feelings of stress, so a better quality thought to note down would be:

I am planning how to get my work done so I still have time to relax this week.

This approach puts your mind in a more proactive mode. It is written in the present tense and is actively working on the issue. This kind of approach will help you feel better about the situation instantly while you are in the process of creating a solution.

Tuesday 7th
Main Thought Of The Day:

I ate too much at lunchtime again instead of going to the gym. I have been worried about it all day. Why do I do this?

Coach Approach

Behind this thought is guilt. Instead of choosing to feel guilty about not working out, simply accept that today wasn't as good as it could have been. A more positive thought would be:

The thought of going to the gym at lunchtime is not at all motivating. Now I am exercising in the morning to get me going first thing!

Again this is in the present tense and includes a solution. Always forgive yourself for not doing what you had intended to do but focus on making tomorrow a better day.

Wednesday 8th
Main Thought Of The Day:

Today I spent time thinking about buying new clothes and daydreaming about a summer vacation, neither of which I can really afford!

Coach Approach

There is nothing wrong with daydreaming as it reconnects us with our subconscious mind and our creativity. What is not so good, however, is feeling guilty about it. A daydream is also a form of escapism and this is something we all need now and again. Perhaps a better quality thought would be:

What a great daydream! If that is what I want, then I am saving and planning for them now.

If you find yourself daydreaming, forget what you were taught as a child about how wasteful it is and indulge in it, because daydreaming is actually good for you!

Thursday 9th
Main Thought Of The Day:

I am never able to get on well with my sister. I love her but she drives me crazy. We are so different that I sometimes think she must have been adopted!

Coach Approach

It isn't always easy to get on with our family. If you have an annoying relative or two, think about how you can improve the situation a little bit at a time. Sometimes, even a different, more positive and loving approach can make all the difference.

This is better than falling into old and destructive scenarios and routines every time you get together. A better thought would be:

It is amazing how different sisters can be. The more I see how different we are, the more I am learning about her and myself.

Friday 10th
Main Thought Of The Day:

I am tired of being treated like a slave at work. My boss is ignorant and I feel I am going nowhere with my career.

Coach Approach

When we are *reacting* to life instead of being *proactive*, we quickly become frustrated. A positive and more constructive way to think about this situation is to assess what skills you need to work on or which ones you need to acquire. Is it a communication problem? If so, think about how you can fix it. A better quality thought would be:

My career needs my attention, so I am putting time aside to think about what opportunities I have both in my current job and elsewhere.

Take a step back and try not to take things personally. Think outside your issues as often as you can. Think about how you can make moves to change and improve your immediate, as well as your long-term, environment.

After about a week or so of using your journal you will get used to checking in with your thoughts and adjusting them to more positive ones. In time, you will create a great new habit of thinking more positively most of the time.

Review of Stage One:

You have reached the end of Stage One of the system and have come a long way. There is a stage review to complete before going on to Stage Two. It is essential that you take the time to go through these questions because they will give you further insights into what you have learned and how much you have grown. You deserve to acknowledge this, so go through them and see for yourself what you have accomplished.

Read the following questions and write the answers in your journal:

1.   What did you learn about happiness from Stage One?

2.   What did you learn about yourself?

3.   Did anything surprise you about what you learned?

4.   Did anything surprise you about the answers you gave to the questions?

5.   What habits or thoughts will you change after completing this stage if any?

Stage Two

The Happiness Myths

'When one door of happiness closes, another opens; but often we look so long at the closed door that we do not see the one which has been opened for us.' **Helen Keller**

In this second stage you will learn the following:

- The common happiness myths we fall for
- How you can rid yourself of them for good
- How to dispel your emotional fears & phobias
- How to identify and dissolve your emotional bad habits
- The truth about having it all

Myths are usually invented stories that have been passed on over time. The myths I am talking about in this stage are those we teach each other about happiness. Happiness myths can be passed on to us by our parents, peers, teachers, friends, lovers and by society in general. I have split these happiness myths into two categories, the first is general myths and the second is absolute lies. General myths: These are misguided beliefs or attitudes about what happiness is. They include common beliefs like having a good job will make you completely happy. The second category is absolute lies. These come from people who are unhappy and want to make others feel bad and so say cruel things. We are susceptible to believing both if we are vulnerable in any way. Our vulnerability comes from either not knowing any better or by suffering from low self-esteem. What we believe we live through and pass on to our children. This is how myths get recycled over again and why many people suffer from unhappiness. I believe that the biggest myths around today are about how to be happy. There are so many about what happiness is and how to get it, its not surprising that generation after generation struggle.

The truth is happiness can be yours. In fact you are already on your way to creating it. However, I want to put a spotlight on these happiness myths so you can rid yourself of them once and for all. I am going to show you in which myths women usually search for happiness, so you can see for yourself why they are not necessarily the right places. Essentially, you will learn what you don't need to worry about when it comes to being happy.

The Most Common Happiness Myths
& How To Overcome Them

First, let's expose some of the most common myths about happiness. Some of the following examples may resonate with you as you recognize which myths you have been buying into. Have no fear! Shattering these myths will be enlightening for you. All you have to do is work through this stage with the knowledge that you are going to learn something new and important about yourself.

Myth One: 'I don't deserve to be happy.'

One of my personal missions in life is to blast this myth right out of the water once and for all. Although it's one myth few confess to believing, far too many of us do. Why is that? Well we usually believe this nonsense because somebody somewhere at one time or another has told us that we are stupid, dumb or useless, i.e. undeserving. As I mentioned earlier, unhappy people say mean things to make others feel bad. Unfortunately, we rarely question what others say about us when we are young or feel vulnerable. This is especially true if it is said to us by a figure in authority. Their lie becomes our fact and repeated exposure to it melts a person's self-esteem. No one wakes up one morning and says, 'I don't deserve to be happy.' A seed is planted first. The truth is, believing that you don't deserve happiness means you are buying into a myth.

The result of believing such a myth causes us to abandon hope of ever being happy. We dismiss the responsibility of creating happiness for ourselves believing happiness is simply out of our control. It's like blaming the cosmos for our fortune. Relinquishing the responsibility of becoming happy is a common mistake. In truth, happiness is a gift. It is a gift from yourself to yourself.

Let me tell you now that *everyone* deserves happiness, especially you. Being happy is not just for a select lucky few, it is for *every* woman.

Myth Blasting Exercise

If you feel that you don't deserve to be happy, I would like to propose the following challenge:

1. Copy the diagram on the next page and write down in your journal ten reasons why you think you don't deserve to be happy.

2. Next to that list, write ten reasons why you think you *do* deserve happiness.

You may or may not reach ten in either list. If you become stuck, simply stop and study what you have written. Take your time to come up with as many as you can. Dig deep. I want you to use all of your reasons, especially those for not deserving happiness.

Exercise Tip: Write as much as you can. Let it flow from the inside. Try not to think too much about what you are going to write. Avoid intellectualizing your reasons, instead let them come from your inner-self.

Why I don't deserve to be happy (negative)	Why I deserve to be happy

Check each list for contradictions. We are not always aware that we have opposing beliefs. If you have any such entries, delete the negative one.

The next part of the exercise is a truth challenge:

3. Take your negative list and mark each entry with a T or an F. The T means *True* and the F means *False*. Decide from your heart if the entry you have made is in fact a true belief or a false belief you have adopted from someone else.

Marking your answers this way gives you an opportunity to contemplate what you have written. This can be a highly emotional exercise, but it's important that you do try to complete it to the best of your ability.

4. Next, delete from your list any entry that you have marked with an F.

Now you have a list of supposedly truthful reasons why you don't deserve to be happy. Read them out loud one by one. Do any of them sound ridiculous to you when you do this? If they do, delete them too. Look at what is left. Is there a connection between them? Check to see if there is a pattern or common factor. If there is, write it down. This will prove to be a useful insight into your beliefs and emotional circumstances. Ask yourself: what can I glean from it? What does this show me?

Out of any remaining beliefs, which is your main reason for not deserving happiness? Look at it and see it for what it really is, a major lie and the main self-imposed barrier to your happiness. You don't have to believe this anymore. Turn it inside out or replace it altogether with a new belief.

As you go through this book, you may want to come back to any remaining reasons for a review session. But I do hope you have managed to delete the entire negative list. As you know, lies cannot hold water under close scrutiny. The reasons you have left are lies. Soon you will believe that too. As you go through each stage you will grow more confident and your negative thoughts and beliefs will be abandoned and replaced by more empowering and enlightened ones.

Myth Two: 'I am only happy in a relationship.'

There is still an enormous amount of pressure from society for women to be part of a couple. True, life is a little easier now for singles. Indeed there has been a growth in the number and type of businesses that purely market to single women. However, being single or divorced is a label that we adopt like a title or identity. Many women are proud to be single and gamely enjoy the freedom it brings, while others agonize over their predicament. Even though it is more acceptable in society, being single at any age can cause a great deal of anxiety.

Ironically, women are the main offenders of this grief. We can be very hard on each other as we sometimes see single women as a threat to our own happiness and security.

Where do you stand when it comes to this myth? Do you believe that happiness is based on being in a relationship? Many do. We believe it because we see so much happiness in a loving, intimate relationship. Of course, being loved and giving love in return is vital for the human soul, but just how happy can we be between relationships? And how can you find that loving relationship?

My answer is that we all have a certain journey in life which is different from anyone else's. Throughout our journey we need to learn and grow as much as possible in order to reap life's outstanding rewards. If you find yourself without a partner at any one time, or if you are in a poor relationship, it is because you have some growing to do that you must complete on your own. It does not mean you are not good enough for a relationship or that there is no one out there for you. It simply means you need to be ready for them. In the right relationship you can continue to grow because it will be more nurturing.

Wherever you are right now in your journey, either with someone or without, is absolutely perfect for you at this time. This is something you have to trust. When the right partner arrives, and they will, the timing will be perfect.

The myth of only being happy while in a relationship can be damaging for women. This is because the fear of being alone may push us into staying in an unhealthy relationship. The supposed security of being with someone is highly desirable, but can lead us into living in a distressing and destructive environment. If this is how it is for you, you can kiss true happiness goodbye. It is choosing a life of compromise and false security. It may seem impossible right now to be without this person, but I can only encourage you to have faith and be brave. Better things are waiting but you have to put yourself in a position where you are able to accept them.

True happiness comes from being true to yourself. Believe that you deserve and will have a great relationship soon. Embrace the time you spend alone and get to know yourself better. Once you know and love yourself more, you are more open and able to receive better things such as a loving relationship.

'I believe that in our constant search for security we can never gain any peace of mind until we secure our own soul.' **Margaret Chase Smith**

Real-Life Story
Shelley is a fun-loving, popular girl who is never short of male admirers. However, she told me that her relationships with men have always been chaotic. When she finally decided to settle down she found that her marriage suffered from a lot of friction. Shelley wondered what was wrong with her and asked me why all her relationships had suffered from the same problem. She wanted to stay in the marriage even though it was painful because she liked the security.

The Coach Approach
Shelley has already decided her future. She has chosen security over true happiness.

Unfortunately, this scenario is all too common. It seems some people will compromise a great deal just to have a feeling of security. Of course, making sacrifices of such magnitude condemns us to live a cheerless life. We may try to ignore how it makes us feel, but it never leaves us. This is because we are living a lie.

To help Shelley, I needed to get to the truth. Deep down she was trying to convince herself that she just wanted to get settled and have a quiet life. The truth was, she wanted the answers to her succession of feeble relationships. I explained the fact that getting to the truth may well turn her life upside down, so she had to be prepared for this.

We started talking about her past relationships. What emerged was her realization that she longed for someone to make her happy. She believed that she could only be happy when she had a man in her life. This explained why she had gone from one relationship to another without any time alone in between. As each relationship failed, she grew more and more frantic about finding Mr. Right, the guy who would make all her dreams come true. When things went wrong she dived straight into the arms of the next seemingly suitable candidate. Time went on so that when she did decide to get married she saw it as a way out of her bad dating experiences.

The Result

During our coaching sessions, Shelley realized that she had been attracting men she had wanted to save, change or fix. Instead of spending time alone to get to know herself more, she spent her time and energy trying to make her boyfriends happy with the belief that they would make her happy in return. Big mistake!

This new insight changed her life. She spent the next few weeks talking with her husband about what she had learned and how she felt about it. They both had to come to terms with their relationship issues but were committed to improving them. It was a new beginning with a new perspective for them. What had seemed hopeless at first now looked hopeful. Instead of looking to each other for happiness, they looked within themselves with the view of being a couple comprised of two well-balanced individuals.

Last time I checked, both Shelley and her husband were doing fine.

How To Dispel Your Emotional Fears & Phobias

'Life's challenges are not supposed to paralyze you, they're supposed to help you discover who you are.' **Bernice Johnson Reagan**

Eliminating emotional fears and phobias is great for taking back the controls of your life. Such feelings can paralyze our ability to be happy because we dare not risk being hurt. Take a look at your approach to being single. How does it affect your life?

This next exercise is very valuable whether you are single or not. Copy the tables overleaf into your journal and complete the exercises before moving onto the next myth.

Fears and Phobias Table

1. Begin by writing down your fears about being in a relationship. For example, do you fear intimacy or being hurt?

2. Write down your fears about being single. What is your worst case scenario? Feeling lonely?

Habit Hazards Table

In this table (on page 62) write down any behavior patterns you have or have had, with past or present partners. For example, do your relationships always end the same way? Do you find that you always argue about the same issues?

Discovering what fears you have when it comes to relationships or being single, is the key to the relationship you have with yourself.

Fears and Phobias

My fears of being in a relationship	My fears when it comes to being single

Habit Hazards

My poor relationship patterns	The main issues I argue about

The next two exercises can be real eye-openers because they expose your negative patterns of behavior. It is important to be aware of your fears so you can overcome them. You need a healthy relationship with yourself before you can create happiness. It doesn't have to be the perfect relationship, just an open and honest one. This means basing all the decisions that you make about life on love for yourself rather than on your fears. Your key to great relationships is to love yourself first and be free of any emotional fears or phobias.

It is important to pay attention to how you treat others and how you let others treat you. This is because it directly mirrors how you treat yourself. If you treat yourself with love, consideration and respect it will become the experience you have in all your relationships. Take time to examine your current relationships and how they affect you. Expose your behavior patterns and fears. Once you have highlighted them, you can begin to heal them and go on to enjoy better quality relationships with friends, loved ones and of course, yourself.

Go back to the Fears and Phobias table. Examine what you wrote and answer the following:

- Where do these fears come from?
- What past experiences have created the beliefs you have today?
- What is your biggest fear?
- How is this affecting your life?
- How would you prefer to feel?
- What would make that perfect?
- What would you have to change in order to reach that goal?
- What can you do today to take you one step closer to it?
- Where might you get stopped?
- What kind of support would be helpful?

Next, go to your Habit Hazards table. Again, look at what you have written and answer the following:

- What, if anything, stands out about your answers?
- What is the main issue for you?
- What do you want the most right now?
- How can you get it?
- What is your role in achieving it?
- What is your vision of a perfect relationship?
- What is your role in achieving it?
- How can you move closer to your vision?
- How can you simplify the process?
- What can you decide about it right now?

These questions are designed to get you to think dynamically about your fears, phobias and habits. Rather than thinking negatively about them, answer the above questions to start moving forward.

Myth Three: 'A great career will make me happy.'

Not necessarily! Many people pursue a career and put their self-worth and identity into what they do for a living. Being successful at what you do for a living is a great personal achievement, but your success will not make you completely happy. I know many people who have excelled at work but are unhappy underneath.

A truly great career is doing a job you love to do, one that you are passionate about. Many pursue a certain career path because they think they should or feel pressure to do so. In the same vein, it is quite common to move from one job to the next searching for a place in life. In each scenario, we can easily map out our whole life without ever really contemplating what we really want to do for a living.

I have coached many professional women who wanted to change their occupation. Most had a deep desire to do something else with their lives that was a million miles away from what they were doing before. They had all been successful but no longer wanted to compromise their happiness. Instead they wanted a job they truly loved, even if it meant giving up everything they had worked very hard for. As you know, this was my story too. This dramatic, yet courageous act proved to me that if you are not being true to yourself you cannot be really happy. To those women, finding their true vocation was far more valuable to them than their status. They were willing to risk it in order to be happy.

Choosing the right career from the beginning is not always an easy task. We have to make important choices early on in life. It is a great shame that many of us don't pursue our dream job right from the start. But few of us actually know what it is. We put so much pressure on ourselves, and often allow others to do the same, that we rarely give ourselves enough time to think about our ideal career. A lucky few know from kindergarten age what they want to do when they grow up. Take my elder sister for example; she was born to be a teacher. It was obvious. She knew it and so did we. But it was not so evident for me or my younger sister. Our true vocations came to us later on in life. How is it for you? Where are you when it comes to career fulfillment? Are you fulfilled? What would you really like to do?

Happiness and career success can go hand in hand. First you have to be clear about your own personal definition of what a successful career is. Being clear about it is another step towards being true to yourself. If you get clear, then you can have a career that helps you to reach your full potential. It is a tragic waste if you don't because happiness means being a success at being you. If you fall into the category of someone who has a certain career because you thought you *should*, know that your dream job is still obtainable. Keep the idea alive in your mind, even if you think changing your vocation seems impossible right now. Don't give up on it. If you really want it, you will find a way to make it happen. The goal setting section later in this book will help you with this. Your dream job does not have to be about saving the world. It just needs to be something you are passionate about. Remember, never feel guilty about want you want to do with your life at any stage in your life. Ignore other people's opinions about what you should or should not do. Always do what you feel is right and never compromise your life. This life is the only one you have, so go all out to make it great.

Myth Blasting Exercise
The following True or False exercise has been designed to help you get a clear idea of where you stand on the career issue. Check which directly apply to your situation:

- My work is a very important part of my life but is not my whole life. *True or False?*

- I feel that I am in the right career for me. *True or False?*

- I do not have a conflict with my home and work life. *True or False?*

- I love every part of my day, everyday. *True or False?*

- I do not let other people's opinions decide how I feel or influence what I do. *True or False?*

Take a look at how many times you have answered 'False.' Be aware of how this affects your life. What will it take for you to answer 'True?' What long-term actions can you take to help you create the ideal situation? Take some form of action right away - no matter how small, to make immediate changes to your current situation.

The Truth About Having It All

One of the big issues for women today who have had, or are thinking of having kids, is whether or not to believe it is possible to have it all. Should you have children *and* work? Do you want to go back to work after having kids or should you stay at home? What does 'having it all' really mean?

Not all women feel that they are in a position to make career choices. Whether we decide to (or have to) go to work, we feel guilty about leaving our children. Some believe that it is impossible to have it all, but what they fail to realize is that 'having it all' has a different meaning for each individual. Forget what the magazine articles say, what does it mean to you?

Often we fall into the trap of trying to be the perfect woman. We want to be the great all-rounder who can turn her hand to anything. This juggling act can make us miserable in the longer-term. Whether you are a mom or not, do you have high standards for yourself? Do you exhaust yourself with trying to be perfect? When it comes to being everything to everyone, which do you try to be?

The perfect mother?

The perfect girlfriend?

The perfect wife?

The perfect independent woman?

The perfect employer?

The perfect employee?

The perfect friend?

It's ok to be perfect at being you. But forget trying to be all things to all people. You decide what you want to be and then enjoy being it. Having it all means doing what you want to on your own terms.

Myth Four: 'Being thin and more attractive will make me happy.'

Discerning women today are extremely knowledgeable about self-development, or *inner*-beauty, as we sometimes call it. Still, we agonize over our looks, or *outer*-beauty, as we continue to buy into society's ideal of how we should look. Even though we know real beauty comes from within, we are spending more money on beauty products and services (including plastic surgery) than ever before. Our self-esteem and confidence remains trapped within the outer-beauty bubble. We buy products and services believing they will make us feel better about ourselves as we close the gap between vanity and self-care. We have become more self-conscious about our weight, breasts, wrinkles and age than ever before.

There are women who are proud of their beauty beliefs and readily admit to the products and treatments they buy. At the other end of the scale, there are women who would never dream of buying anything more sophisticated than lip balm. Even when there is a diversity of beliefs among women about beauty, we all share a common struggle and that is with our inner-critic.

Question yourself about this topic. Answer the following questions to discover what you really believe:

- Is inner-beauty just an ideal?
- How do you judge your beauty?
- What is your best feature?
- What is your worst?
- How much do your looks affect how you feel?
- What is *real* beauty to you?
- What is the truth about how you feel inside?

We conform in thought and action to a deep image of ourselves. If we don't change a negative self-image we will never think of ourselves as attractive enough.

We either create a self-image that can support and nurture happiness or have a negative one that constantly deflates us. Think about it for a moment. It is very important for you to be aware of how you really feel about yourself both inside and out.

The beauty products we buy are never supposed to work for us on the inside, yet many industries focus on producing merchandise or services that are aimed at making women happy. How far do we rely on them? Is that what happiness actually is…a product? If so, can happiness be bought after all?

The answer of course is a resounding NO! Buying a facial is one thing, but think carefully about what else you buy to feel happy. Why does it make you feel happy? What need does the item or service actually satisfy?

We know that outer-beauty can be bought and we know that it's our inner-beauty that counts. Why then do we still worry and get stressed about how we look? At what level does outer-beauty matter? What is the difference between what we claim we want and what we really want when it comes to beauty? And when we look in the mirror who exactly are we comparing ourselves to?

Being physically attractive may bring you more attention but it certainly does not make you happy. But how do we make that switch from knowing it intellectually to understanding it emotionally?

Outer-beauty fades with time. While there is nothing wrong with taking pride in our bodies, it is unhealthy to abuse ourselves because we don't feel we fit in to society's idea of what beauty is. When we have low self-esteem, we tend to use our body as a target. We make ourselves sick through obsessive dieting, exercise or binge eating. The pressure we feel to be thin and attractive is enormous and often overpowering. It starts when we are young and if we let it, it continues throughout our life. Unfortunately, too few women love or believe in themselves enough not to be influenced by this pressure. This is why inner-beauty is essential. I encourage you to keep a healthy beauty balance by continuing to develop your self-esteem, self-acceptance and self-love throughout your life.

Myth Blasting Exercise

Make a decision to be kinder and more loving to yourself. Don't scrutinize your appearance. Do take care of yourself in a more nurturing and less punishing way. Feel good about yourself. And know that this takes patience, understanding, emotional intelligence and love.

Do not compare how you look with other women. Happiness has nothing to do with appearance. Many magazines or other forms of media portray an extreme version of women. We come in all shapes and sizes so embrace *your* form. Real beauty is the confidence that comes with accepting who we are lovingly and thoroughly. Give yourself a break and just be who you are without any nagging doubts of being attractive enough.

Focus on this for at least one month. Take a note of how many times you having feelings of inadequacy. Become more aware of the media messages out there and how they make you feel. Think behind the messages. What is being portrayed as beautiful? How does this affect you as a woman?

Change your beliefs about outer-beauty so you start to think about it in a less emotional way. This will make it easier for you to see your real inner-beauty in its unique form. Once you see it, you can accept it and love it. Decide to shine from the inside out and stop worrying about looking right. The self-confidence you will develop will give you a special glow that others will find very attractive.

Take time to notice other women. Look at those you know and those who just happen to pass by. What is attractive about them? Also, practice looking in the mirror with a less critical eye. Start to notice the beauty in your eyes and smile. See beyond your body into your soul to where your real beauty lies.

Other Myths We Buy Into:

'I am too old to be happy.'

Age is a wonderful excuse for many things both good and bad. Examples of the bad include: being too old to have fun, being too old to change, being too old to fall in love or being too old to be happy. How old you are has *nothing* to do with being happy. It's all about your state of mind. Some of us allow ourselves to become old before our time. We actually believe we are washed up at forty or past it in our thirties! This is madness! We seem to live in a youth obsessed culture that fears aging. The truth is older women should be admired because they have lived more.

We have the benefit of being younger longer these days because we choose to marry and have children much later on in life. This leaves us more time to be youthful. But youthfulness is a state of mind, so choose what you want to be. If you choose to let your feelings about your age dictate what you can or cannot do, then you are creating big limitations for yourself. If on the other hand, you choose to ignore how old you are, you can embrace life fully and enjoy every stage. Age becomes unimportant when you are busy fulfilling your life's dream as it can bring wonderful and unexpected gifts. So remember you are never too old to be happy regardless of how old you may feel.

'Having a big house and lots of money will make me happy.'

Sure, having money to buy whatever you want can make you feel good. However, as you know, money cannot buy you happiness. Don't believe it will be different for you. Possessions don't make us happy. Shopping can make us feel great, but it's a short-term pleasure. In fact buying material things is usually a substitute for happiness. Craving things like expensive cars, clothes, jewelry and big houses is buying into the myth that they have a special value. You may have heard it said that if a house is burning down, the one thing that people try and rescue is their family photographs. This proves that when the heat is on, life's more expensive accessories do not matter. If we are unhappy, we may buy material goods to make us feel we are worth something but we are merely attempting to fill a void. Having glamorous possessions can be fun and I believe that we should all enjoy them just so long as we see them as toys or accessories to life and not happiness itself.

Money often acts like a magnifying glass. The more money we have, the more it magnifies our current situation. If you are happy, having more money will make you feel happier, but if you are unhappy, having more money will merely magnify that too. Often people confuse being happy with financial wealth. There is nothing wrong with money, but its real value should be put into perspective. Having it allows us to buy things, but it is not a way to happiness, it is an *addition* to happiness. I personally believe in a balance in all things and so my own philosophy in life is to create wealth in all areas of my life, not just financially.

'Eating makes me happy.'

For some of us, food has more functions than mere nourishment. Indeed food can be used as a comfort and a shield against the world. Eating does not bring us happiness, but it can temporarily make us feel good. We can subconsciously abuse food and use it as a substitute for things that we lack like love for example. We have to think about food every day so there are ample opportunities for us to indulge. Throughout each day we have to make decisions about food, therefore, it is not surprising that sometimes our emotions become involved in our eating decisions. We substitute feelings and sometimes relationships with food. The result is that we often eat, or do not eat, because of our emotional attachment to food.

It is perfectly fine to indulge in our favorite foods now and again, but when we overeat, or starve ourselves, we have emotional issues that should not be ignored. Too many women suffer from food related disorders. If we can take the emotion out of eating and keep it as something to enjoy and not reward or punish ourselves with, we have a chance of being happier. Sometimes we adopt or develop bad food habits, so if you suffer from a poor relationship with food, get to the bottom of the issue by asking yourself the following questions:

- What do I want from food?

- How do I use food?

- How do I feel when I am eating?

- How do I feel after I have eaten?

- How often do I think about food each day?

- How often do I eat something which I think is bad for me?

- What kind of food is off limits for me?

- What did my parents teach me about food?

- What do I teach, or what will I teach my kids about food?

- What would be my ideal relationship with food?

- How close am I to this ideal relationship?

- How can I move even closer to it?

Take time to consider your answers, as they may reveal a lot. Getting an accurate picture of your relationship with food will help you improve your situation, no matter where you are starting from. Denial is our worst enemy when it comes to creating happiness. Be honest about where you can make changes or create new habits. If you think you have a bad relationship with food don't be ashamed or afraid to ask for help.

The Two Biggest Happiness Lies Ever

There are two big happiness myths we tell ourselves and these are:

I tried my best to be happy but…

and

You cannot control your own destiny.

The first myth explains why many of us just give up trying to be happy. People who believe this cannot see how they are ever going to be happy and are exhausted trying. Of course, when this happens it is a clear sign that they have been *looking* for happiness. Their futile search has led them to believe that happiness is not for them because they have tried and failed. They don't get that happiness is created and not found.

The second myth is a toughie. We are so fond of this we actually embrace it. But it is not strictly true. We *do* have a say in how our life unfolds because as I have explained earlier our thoughts create our reality. True, there are some things we cannot control, but for the most part, the decisions and choices we make map out our future.

There are many other happiness myths that I haven't mentioned, like why we believe being important or famous means being happy. What I have aimed to do here is give you a good idea of the type of myths that surround us every day and how powerful and controlling they can be.

Think about what other happiness myths exist and become aware of how easily they can influence you.

Ask yourself why that is. Set out to become an expert on these myths so you can avoid them from now on. Always question what people are saying to you about happiness. They may be coming from a very different set of circumstances and background. Know what is genuinely true about happiness for you and stick with it.

Review of Stage Two

Congratulations on reaching the end of Stage Two! Again, to get the most out of this stage and the happiness system, review what you have learned:

1. What myths were you buying into?

2. Have you made any major, or even minor, decisions about your life because of what you have learned?

3. What will you do differently from now on?

4. Do you have a better understanding of what true happiness is?

5. Describe it.

6. For you, what one thing stood out the most in this stage?

7. What will you do today, tomorrow, the next day and so on to help create more happiness for yourself?

Stage Three

Your Map To Happiness

'Living a life is like constructing a building: if you start wrong, you'll end wrong.'
Maya Angelou

In this third stage you will learn the following:

- The eight elements of happiness
- How to calculate how happy you are right now
- How you can improve your happiness score
- How this will impact your life
- How to prioritize your happiness elements

This stage gives you a unique opportunity to measure your Happiness Quotient (HQ), which illustrates how happy you are right now. We will work through each of the eight elements associated with happiness so you can calculate your total happiness score. The aim is to get the highest score possible as the higher the score, the happier you are! I have devised The Happy Map exercise to include all areas of life from the practical to the spiritual. Take one element at a time and create a picture of where you are right now and compare it with where you would like to be. Happy mapping is a great coaching tool that I have adapted specifically for you. Learning to coach yourself this way will help you to become more effective in creating happiness and harmony in your life. I will not only guide you through each area in turn, but will also give you extra tips and detailed information about each element. Once you have completed the Happy Map, you will clearly see which areas of your life need your attention. There may be some surprises along the way as this exercise also helps you to discover where your real strengths lie. You can make an enormous amount of progress during this stage, so enjoy it and happy learning!

The Happy Map

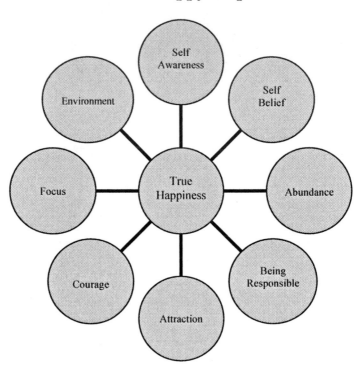

How To Navigate The Happy Map

There are eight happiness elements. Each one requires your attention and two separate scores. This is how it works:

1. First, re-draw the above diagram in your journal.

2. Next, take each section in turn and read the notes about it in the Eight Elements of Happiness section.

3. Once you have a clear idea of what the element is about, go back to your Happy Map and give yourself a score between one and ten (ten being high). This score should illustrate where you are right now.

4. Then, put in a second score next to your first. This depicts the score you would *like* to have in that area. This will probably be a ten.

If in part 3 you give yourself a score of six or below, it means that the area needs some attention. A score between seven and nine indicates that a little more work is required in that area, but it is not necessarily a priority for you right now. If you gave yourself a score of ten in any of the elements, then you have it under control and can focus on another area for now.

The Eight Elements Of Happiness

1. Self-Awareness

How well do you know yourself? Biblical advice like, 'know thyself' is as ancient as it is true because being aware of exactly who you are is vital to your level of happiness. We have already discussed self-awareness when it comes to needs and yearnings and so the next step is having the ability to distinguish between your authentic-self and your ego. Your authentic-self is the soft voice of your heart and soul, whereas your ego, or inner-critic, is the loud, negative and discouraging voice. These voices are communicating to us all the time. Voices?! Sounds crazy doesn't it? Let me explain. The truth is we talk to ourselves all the time. As I mentioned earlier, your mind is constantly having internal conversations and producing thoughts. Some we are aware of and others are subconscious. The art of happiness is to turn down the volume of the booming voice of our ego, and turn up the volume of the quiet inner-voice of our authentic-self. Learn to recognize your inner-voice. Listen to it. It is wise and caring while your ego is not. Your authentic voice believes you can achieve anything you want to, whereas your ego does not. Guess which voice we listen to most of the time?! The ego echoes our fears and so listening to it prevents us from doing what we truly want to in life. Our egos also gossip, whine, make excuses and blame others for our own misfortune. The only real power it has is the actual volume at which we hear it.

Mastering self-awareness involves practice. Practice listening to your authentic self. The best way to do this is to be still and quiet. Meditation and relaxation exercises help. Listening to your authentic voice is an uncomplicated process. Simply sit somewhere undisturbed for at least 10 minutes and start to listen. To help, ask yourself a question about your life or ask for guidance. Listen to the answer and let yourself be guided by it. Ignore your ego's attempts at being heard, listen below the noise.

Your authentic self is also described as your intuition. So learn to develop a strong connection with it. It will always guide you in the right direction. The answers to your questions may not always come straight away, but they will come.

Before you give yourself a score in this element, go through these questions to get a better idea of how self-aware you are:

- What does your ego tell you most of the time?
- How well has your ego served you so far in life?
- Have you been aware of your authentic voice before now?
- If yes, what kind of things does it say to you?
- If you have ever followed its guidance, how did it make you feel?

Answering the first two questions will help you make a further distinction between your ego and your authentic self. They highlight the messages your ego sends to you and how you may or may not benefit from them. The next three questions concentrate on your authentic self and its messages. The final question focuses on your feelings towards it. It's important for you to acknowledge this.

Now rate your level of self-awareness on the map. At the same time think how you can improve your score. Remember that becoming self-aware takes practice and dedication, so regularly take the time to tune into your inner-self. I know that listening to it will give you amazing inner-strength, wisdom, confidence and inner-peace.

Extra Info:
Stage Four is dedicated to the important issue of 'Personal Power.' You will learn how to tap into your own abundant inner-resources quickly and effectively. It is powerful stuff and will change your life.

2. Self-Belief

This is one of the most important aspects of being happy and requires a lot of focus. Believing in yourself is the key to having a great life. A life where you get to *do* everything you want, *see* everything you want and *be* everything you want. You cannot make significant progress in life without a strong belief in yourself.

We are born with our self-belief intact yet it can be often weakened or even destroyed by something or someone in our life. Very few adults manage to reach their thirties with their self-belief still going strong. People will continue to suffer from having a low self-esteem if they are not educated on how to counteract damage and rebuild their sense of worth.

Women particularly experience a lack of self-belief because of our tendency to compare and judge ourselves against others. Self-depreciating thoughts result in poor decision-making and outcomes. Work on improving your level of self-belief like your life depended on it, because it does. Then every other area of your life will improve.

Let's take a good look at how you see yourself. Ask yourself the following:

- What do I think about when I think about myself?
- What are my greatest strengths?
- What do I need to focus on?
- What do I like about myself?
- Do I believe I am capable of achieving anything I want to?
- If not, why not?

In question one, it may be helpful to use metaphors to express how you feel. For example you can use animals, adverbs or colors to give it an added dimension. Notice that the third question asks you what you need to focus on. I do not mention your weaknesses because thinking about those is a waste of time. Besides, I would like you to start being very aware of the words you use from now on. To help you experience a better life, you need to use more positive and empowering language. I shall be covering this in more detail in Stage Five. To answer the third question thoroughly, write as much down as you can. Again, make sure that what you write is true for you and not an adopted belief from somewhere else. Next, highlight what you think are your top three and forget the rest for now. There are two reasons for this; firstly, pinpointing your main areas of focus helps you to start working on them straight away. Secondly, if you focus on just three, then you don't overwhelm yourself by thinking about too many! Focus on expanding upon question four as much as possible. Answering the fifth question will give you an insight into how competent you think you are. Also, you get to think about what you would like to achieve in life. This gives you an opportunity to think about the greatest thing you dare do and see how you rate your abilities in accomplishing it. Think of another goal and repeat the exercise. Do this again and again, lowering the challenge rating of your goal until you get to one that would only be slightly challenging for you. What you have created is a list of what you want to achieve along with a self-appraised possibility rating. Pick one of your easier goals and a more challenging one. Set a timescale for achieving them both. Be as realistic as possible but not pessimistic. Ask yourself what you will have to do each day, week, month or year to achieve them. Focus on them every day and reward your progress no matter how insignificant. You should complete your easy goal quickly. This will start a powerful mental process that will make you feel able to tackle a more challenging goal. As you achieve one goal after the other you will build momentum and start to see yourself achieving things you never thought possible. This sense of ability, competence and determination will drive you forward as your self-belief grows.

Knowing what you want and how to get it are essential in creating happiness. When you go all out to achieve your goals in good faith and by harming no one, you are adding great things to the world. You are helping others see that it is possible to achieve dreams. Can you imagine a world where everyone is working towards their dreams? You will be able to learn more about goal setting in Stages Four and Six. Answer the following:

- How do you rate your level of self-belief overall?
- What score are you aiming for?
- What can you do today to improve your score?

You can improve how you feel about yourself starting today. Believe that you can do anything you want to. There is no such thing as failure. Understand that making mistakes means you are learning and this is what life is all about.

3. Abundance

This element is probably the most fun and takes the least amount of work. It is simply to know and understand that we live in a generous and abundant world. Let's go through the principles behind abundant thinking so you can give yourself a score. Believing in a world of abundance means you believe that the world wants you to be happy. You believe that there is plenty of love, happiness and wealth for everyone. Essentially, you are buying into the belief of a loving, generous and giving world. Too many of us believe in scarcity, the exact opposite of abundance. Scarcity thinking is believing that the good things in life are in short supply. Beliefs like this create a substantial negative impact on our lives. If you really believe that there is not enough happiness in this world to go around, then you can easily rationalize why you are not happy. Many people use scarcity as an excuse for their unhappiness. The truth is they have not yet found their way to abundant thinking. I have heard people say that if you want to be happy then just be happy. However, I know from experience it is a little more involved than that. Issues need to be healed and minds need to be enlightened first. It is your attitude towards the world, however, that is one of the most significant keys to happiness. Answer these questions about your outlook on life:

- How do you rate your approach to the world?
- Do you believe in an abundant world or one of scarcity?
- If scarcity rules your world, how well has that attitude worked for you so far?
- What will you do to improve this?

Changing an attitude that has only resulted in negative outcomes for you is a great opportunity to make lasting life improvements. Let go and acknowledge the power of changing your mind. As women, changing our minds is our prerogative! Let's face it, it's no fun being right when it means being miserable. Besides, believing in a world of great beauty, resources and love is a better existence. When you truly believe there is great abundance, your world will change for the better. Realize that there is more than enough happiness to go around and stake your claim! Get what you deserve. In an abundant world, being happy creates more happiness, wealth creates more wealth and love creates more love.

4. Being Responsible

'Nothing strengthens the judgment and quickens the conscience like individual responsibility.' **Elizabeth Cady Stanton**

Being responsible for yourself and your actions is a very grown-up thing to do. So why is it that so few adults do it? Domestic responsibilities are different to personal ones. Being responsible for your life and your actions means moving into the driving seat and taking charge. You stop playing the victim and start living knowing that the buck stops with you.

Take charge of who you are and what you do. There is an enormous amount of freedom and joy when you do. Your actions affect your destiny, so being responsible for them is vital. Answer these questions honestly and decide your score for this element:

- How responsible are you?
- How much control do you exercise over your own life?
- Do you always take full responsibility for your actions?
- If not, who do you blame when things go wrong?
- Do you ever take responsibility for the actions of other people?

As ever, see how you can make improvements to your score. Re-adjust any negative thoughts you may have about being responsible. Remember, being responsible is not about being dull, it is about taking charge.

5. Attraction

I would like to tell you about one of the best universal laws there is, the Law of Attraction. It states that what we think about most of the time becomes our reality. In other words, we are living magnets and attract all the things in our lives because of how we think.

Take a moment and think about how your life is today:

- Who is in it?
- What friends do you have?
- What do you spend most of your time doing?
- What kind of relationships do you experience?
- How much does your life reflect the way you think?

As I mentioned earlier, your thoughts are extremely powerful. They determine how you approach the world and how you react to events. They act like a filter through which you view everything. Your inner-world or perspective, creates your reality. Take the saying, 'what goes around comes around' for example. The Law of Attraction is the explanation behind that insight. Whatever energy you send out into the universe will come back to you. Therefore, if you think negatively most of the time you will attract negative experiences.

If that is how attraction works, then it is safe to say that the trick to having more positive experiences is to think more positively. Thinking positively creates a different kind of energy, so changing the way you think can change your life almost immediately. Answer the following:

- Which areas of your life need improving?
- How can you change how you think to improve them?

As you read through this stage you will realize how connected each happiness element is and how by improving one area, you will simultaneously develop the others.

How do you score on attraction? Do you constantly think negatively about yourself, your life and other people? If so, give yourself a low score. If you are usually optimistic and upbeat, give yourself a score of seven or above. Average scores are not ok in this book. Aim high.

Overall, remember that what we attract in life is a direct reflection of how we think. How we think is determined by what we believe to be true. I discussed the importance of beliefs earlier and in Stage Five we will explore them in much greater detail. Then you may want to revisit this section afterwards to re-evaluate your score.

When I use the mapping tool in coaching, I usually suggest that any score of six or below requires attention. A real challenge is when you have a score of seven and want to raise it to a score of ten. This challenge often inspires my clients. If you have a high score in any of the elements, why not challenge yourself to work towards scoring a ten? What do you need to do to score a ten?

This exercise encourages you to take a step away from your emotions and review your life rationally and more spiritually. It also gives you a good idea of what needs to happen in order for you to go from a lower score to score a higher one. Adapt the Happy Map diagram to fit any subject you want. For example, if you want to focus on relationships, take the diagram and mark the eight sections into relevant topics such as; communication, expectations, sex, self-love and boundaries. Then give yourself a score in each area.

I shouldn't really tell you this but I have often done the above relationship exercise with male clients. When we get to the section marked 'sex' they almost always give themselves a high score. Just to be sure, I remind them that the score for this section is not how they rate themselves in bed, but indicates how active their sex life is. After hearing this explanation, they almost always lower their score! Bless them!

6. Courage
'Courage is the price that life exacts for granting peace.' **Amelia Earhart**

Courage is an amazing virtue. You can know everything there is to know, you can even be a self-aware master, but if you lack the courage to take action, then everything you have learned is worthless. Courage is a vital ingredient to the happiness recipe, so take this opportunity to learn more about it and give yourself an accurate score.

In the movie 'The Wizard of Oz,' the wizard points out to Dorothy and her companions that they already had within themselves everything they wanted namely, a brain, a heart and courage. They just didn't realize it. Like the lion, all the courage you will ever need to overcome life's obstacles is already inside of you.

What issues in life are you experiencing right now? Write them down so you can look at them more objectively. It is always tempting for us not to look too closely at our problems in the hope that they might go away. When we do this, there is a chance that the real cause of our anguish may never be resolved.

Courage is about confronting what makes us unhappy and dealing with it. Ignoring our issues will not make them go away. Do not be afraid of emotional pain. It will teach you a lot about yourself. The real pain comes from hiding away.

To get a good idea of where you are now as far as your courage rating is concerned, answer the following questions:

- Have you ever prevented yourself from doing something you really wanted to?
- If so, how has it affected your life?
- What do you do to hide from your problems?
- How does this limit your life?
- What problem or obstacle can you resolve today?

In the fifth question, I encourage you to take action now and start weeding out these issues. Setting a goal like this will develop your courage and give you the confidence to face anything. Be more aware of how courage can help change your life for the better.

By using your courage…

- How much more could you do?
- How much more could you be?
- How much more could you have?
- What have you got to lose?

Go back to the Happy Map. Add your courage score to it and set yourself a goal to improve it by at least two points within the next three months. If you have given yourself a high score then applaud that fact and make sure you acknowledge this great strength of yours.

7. Focus

The power of focus is a marvelous thing. Whatever you focus on holds great energy and the ability to shape your life. Focusing on what you want in a positive way directs your energy and brainpower into attracting it. By using the energy of focus, you literally become a powerhouse of strategy and purpose. Learning how to use your focus is one of the most compelling tools for happiness and life mastery.

The ability to focus on something helps to manifest it into our lives. So be very careful about what you focus on! If you focus on what you don't want, it too could materialize. The energy of focus is potent but it cannot differentiate between something positive and something negative. Decide what you want to focus on and be very aware of where your energy is directed.

Becoming more aware of your focus is simply a matter of being more vigilant. Thinking about where you want to go in life is ideal focus material. Set goals, because working towards them can give you a great sense of purpose, self-worth and a sense of accomplishment. People who do are generally happier. They find it extremely rewarding. If you value your future, you should use your energy to manifest what you want.

Answer the following questions:

- What kind of things do you focus on most?

- How have they manifested themselves into your life?

- What do you want to stop focusing on?

- What do you want to start focusing on?

The first two questions will give you a personal example of how the power of focus works. The third question gives you the chance to re-asses your focusing habits. Once you have written down what you want to stop focusing on, create a Thought Journal to monitor your progress. This will increase your awareness and help you think more about what you do want and less about what you don't want.

8. Environment

The environment element of the Happy Map is about where and how you choose to live. It is an important element that can dictate your overall feelings of happiness. Your every day environment has powerful influences over your comfort, health, progress and success.

Early on in life we have little say about our immediate environment and may have to suffer uncomfortable surroundings. But as adults we have a choice.

The main areas of your environment include:

1. Where you live
2. How you live

3.   Who you are surrounded by
4.   How supportive it is to your development
5.   How it adds to your life
6.   How it takes away from your life
7.   How ideal it is for you

Take time to consider each one of the seven aspects of your environment. How you feel about your environment directly relates to how you feel about yourself. If you have an ideal environment that is beautiful, safe, clean and supportive, then know you deserve it. If however, your environment is lacking in any way, ask yourself what is stopping you from improving it and if that is a valid reason.

Never underestimate the value of your surroundings. If you are working on your inner-self, your outer-environment can play an important part in how successful you are. If you would rather soar with the eagles but instead find yourself scratching around with the chickens, then it is time to improve your environment. It is possible to make quick and effective changes to it.

Have a look around you now and ask yourself the following questions:

- Does my environment please me?

- What can I improve about it today?

- Who or what is missing that would make all the difference?

- Who or what should go?

- Is it a healthy environment?

- Does it contain good role models?

- Do I have room to grow?

- Does it support me?

- How can I improve it over time?

How do you rate your environment today? What's your score? Once you have noted this on the Happy Map, start to make plans for both instant and long-term improvements.

Extra Info:
Our greater environment is as important as our immediate one. World events can have a dramatic and long-lasting effect on our lives. As we have little control over them, it is important to understand their affect on our feelings of wellbeing. Your approach to such events determines how much they affect your happiness. Be hopeful and upbeat, believe the world is a good place and be thankful for its beauty. Do what you can to add to your greater environment.

What's Next?
Now you have completed your scoring on the Happy Map, you should have a good idea of which elements need your attention. Try to improve your scores. To do this, first choose the area you think needs your attention first. This is your priority. It does not necessarily have to be the one with the lowest score. It may be easier for you to start with a section that only requires a small amount of attention.

Next, give yourself a target by aiming to increase your score by three points within a month. Think about what would need to change or improve in your life for you to achieve this. Resist the temptation to try and go from a score of five directly to a score of ten. This may prove too challenging and leave you disappointed. Building up from an easy success will help you make vast improvements in each element quickly and will give you a long-term strategy for improving your life.

That was the practical side of the exercise. The emotional one is in recognizing, and practicing what needs to be done to improve your scores. This is the next stage of goal setting. Having well-defined goals gives you more direction in life and encourages you to focus on making progress every day.

The HQ exercise can be used continually so you are constantly aware of your improvements in each area of your life. It is always worthwhile to come back often to this exercise and review where you are.

Happy Map Footnote

Balancing each element of the Happy Map is important. Make sure each area receives your attention. Maintaining this balance is like juggling hoops. You have to keep all eight in the air at once. If you drop one, i.e. you develop issues in that area, it is a sign that you are neglecting it. It takes practice, but achieving high levels of happiness and balance comes from attending to those areas that need improvement without neglecting the others. Make this level of self- awareness a habit by giving it the time and focus it needs. Soon you will do it naturally and effortlessly.

Review of Stage Three

Now you should have a pretty good idea of where you are in terms of your Happiness Quotient. The top score is 80. How does your total score compare?

Having a better understanding of what elements create happiness and how you score in each is advanced self-awareness and a significant part of The Happiness System. Ensure that you are working towards a better score in each element at all times. Now review what you have learned:

1. What did your learn about the elements of happiness?

2. What did you learn about yourself through your scores?

3. Which element of the Happy Map is your main priority and why?

4. What can you do this week to give yourself a better score in this element?

5. Which element will you look to improve next?

Stage Four

Personal Power

'We evolve only when we participate, not when we sit on the sidelines fearing inadequacy. And the more we act, the more wisdom, confidence, and excellence we receive.' **Jill Badonsky**

In this fourth stage you will learn the following:

- How to tap into your personal power
- What you want from life
- To evaluate your expectations
- The importance of having faith
- The truth about self-sabotage
- What you resist and why
- How to create stronger intentions
- How to use the power of choice

This stage teaches you how to tap into your own personal power. It is here that you will start to make the internal changes to reveal your powerful self. It is time to stop hiding your light or being embarrassed and self-conscious. Let yourself shine and feel the warmth of your inner-glow. You have worked hard to get this far and should be very proud of yourself. This next stage is highly-effective and will open your mind to unlimited personal development.

Are you ready? Ok, this is what we shall be covering: First of all, we are going to look at you, who you are and what you want. Next, we are going to get super smart and assess all the possible pitfalls that could prevent you from succeeding in life. Awareness of them will prevent you from falling into them. Then we will explore your subconscious mind to reveal and cultivate your inner-essence.

Finally, we shall focus on the very things that prevent you from being happy. This includes how your own actions can cause you big set backs. For this stage you will need your journal, the more notes you make the better.

Who Are You & What Do You Want From Life?

What Are You Worth?

Think about your worth as a human being and in your various roles as a woman. How valuable do you think you are? The truth is, we rarely recognize our true value. Besides being highly critical of ourselves, we are also very modest. Even genuine praise from others is often dismissed as just flattery. Our difficulty with accepting how others value us is down to low self-esteem. How do you sincerely accept and love who you are? Start by considering why it's so hard to be kind and compassionate to yourself.

Let's get to the bottom of this self-worth issue. Below is a list of eight character traits most people regard as the essence of worthiness;

These are being...

loving	generous
strong	forgiving
compassionate	wise
patient	helpful

Note that this list does not contain descriptions like; beautiful, smart, talented, competent, successful, rich or well-dressed. Yet these are the attributes we judge our worthiness on.

Concentrate on what really counts and stop doubting whether you are good enough. Realize that you are, always have been and always will be.

Answer the following:

- What do you believe about your own worthiness?

- Of the eight character traits listed earlier, how many can you claim?

Take time to think about your answers. Above all, remember that this is an exercise to improve how you feel about yourself. In Stage Five, I shall help you more with the self-worth issue so you can move on to master self-love.

Who Are You?

In Stage Three we talked about self-awareness, now I want you to think about your make-up. Your inner make-up as opposed to your L'Oreal! What do you *consist* of? Happiness means knowing yourself and not letting other people define you. Go through this next exercise to explore exactly who you are. Write down your answers for each of the following empowering and self-discovery questions. It may take time, but once you have completed them you will have more clarity about your personal dynamics and true self.

Answer the following:

- Who are you from the ground up?
- Where are you coming from?
- How much does your culture influence who you are?
- How free are you?

- Where are you heading in life?
- Where does your energy come from?
- What drives you forward?
- What holds you back?
- What do you let happen?
- What do you *make* happen?

The first three questions get you to reflect upon your personal history, philosophy and attitude. Consider how they have developed over the years and how much they influence you. Resist answering the first question with labels to describe yourself. Don't use words like 'single' or 'married,' for example. Go deeper. Question four asks how free you are. In your answer include how much freedom you allow yourself. Do you believe you are free to do whatever you like? Do you think, move and act freely? The next three questions are about your future. Add to your previous notes. Contemplate the following:

- Compare where you are headed in life to where you would like to go.
- What is making you head in this direction?
- What lies at the very core of who you are?
- How does this affect your reality today?
- What part of yourself do you want to create your reality in the future?

Developing your answers will build a clearer picture of who you are. This in turn will give you more confidence, resolve and peace of mind. Check your answers for any negative connotations or outside influences. Your answers should reflect your true self, not what you have been told about yourself or think are the right answers. You have to be real and get real to communicate from your heart and soul. Have the courage to be totally honest with yourself. This type of commitment is your guarantee to a compelling future.

What Do You Want?

What do you want? What do you really, really want? Use my question as an invitation to self-indulge. In the last stage you thought about what goals you could achieve. If you haven't done this yet, I want you to write a sparkling, inspiring, dreamy, delicious and earth-shattering wish list of what you and you alone want. Ready? Go!

Have you done it? You *must* do it and we shall go no further until you do…..I'm waiting!

Not so easy is it? You think that when you finally get to express what you want in life you wouldn't struggle doing it. Why is that? The answer is simple. We are very rarely, if indeed ever, asked what we want. Consequently, we never get to really think about it. Basically it's a lack of practice.

If you haven't done your list yet, do it now. I want you to take full advantage of this opportunity. Make a wish or two and make them big. Play the role of 'Cinderfairy,' my word for being Cinderella and the Fairy Godmother in one. Not only do you make the wishes, you make them come true too.

Write down whatever wishes come to mind, no matter how ridiculous they may seem. Be careful what you wish for and be exact about what you want. Be wise and think each one through carefully before you commit to it. If you did write goals earlier, make sure they are as exciting as possible.

Now that you have your list, answer the following questions;

- What is at the top of your list?
- Is it your most important wish?
- If not, what is?
- What is your most daring wish?
- What wish do you want to happen first and why?
- Which one do you think is the least likely to happen and why?
- What wishes have you left off the list and why?

Analyzing your list gives you a clear understanding of your heart's true desire. It also gives you the opportunity to ensure that you don't hold out on yourself by neglecting certain wishes. No deeply held wish is silly.

Now that you have breathed life into what you want, the only thing left to do is to make your wishes come true. Before you do, I just want to remind you about guilt. It is not necessary, or indeed helpful, to feel guilty when you are thinking about what you want. Remember, people in your life will be a lot happier when you are a lot happier. Never associate negative feelings with your wishes or feel guilty spending time making them come true.

Magic Wand At The Ready!

The truth behind our love of fairy tales like Cinderella, is our infatuation with magical and enchanting stories. We want to live happily ever after too, yet few of us grow up expecting our lives to be as dreamy. What a shame and how dull and uninspiring! What happened to your dreams? At which point did they vanish into thin air to be replaced by car payments and a mortgage? Re-embrace your dreams and believe they can come true. Use everything you have inside to re-energize your life and live your dream.

Stern Warning to all Cinderfairies:

When it comes to thinking about what you want don't expect a handsome prince to come dashing in heroically and save you. You don't need saving. You have your own magic. You just need more faith in its ability.

Your magic comes from believing in yourself and that what you want will come to you. The world will provide you with everything you want, it's just waiting for you to claim it. Take your wish list and set the cosmic wheels in motion by declaring what you want. Then it's up to you to start using your personal powers to make it materialize.

Your powers include:

- Focus
- Expectations
- Faith
- Ability to ask

We have already discussed 'Focus' in Stage Three, so now we will concentrate on your other three powers; expectations, faith and the ability to ask.

Great Expectations

Your expectations have an enormous amount of power. Like your thoughts, they influence your reality. Answer these questions. Dig deep to unearth whether your expectations are working with you or against you.

Take time to go through the following:

- What are your expectations of life?

- Do you expect to succeed?

- Do you expect to be happy?

- What do you expect of others?

- What do you expect of yourself?

- What beliefs are your expectations based on?

- Have any of your expectations ever been crushed?

- Are any of your expectations adopted from someone else?

- How have your expectations changed over time?

When coaching, asking these types of questions can reveal plenty. The results are often surprising and sprinkled with 'aha!' moments. Coach yourself here and now. Acquire a healthy habit of thinking around the subject. Live more intentionally. Check your expectations regularly and ask yourself:

- Are they positive enough?
- Are they powerful enough?
- Do they support my wishes?

Check to see if some of your expectations are unreasonable. Also check if some don't entirely depend on you for the outcome. Like the goals you set, you have to be the only one responsible for making them happen.

Other People

We can often get badly hurt or disillusioned because of our expectations of other people. It's not necessarily because our expectations are too high, although that can be an issue. It's because we have absolutely no control over what other people do. It is good to have high expectations of people. The problems occur when we expect a person to be someone other than who they are. If we simply expect people to be themselves, then we can never be disappointed.

To expect anyone to change is a futile and frustrating notion. Think and expect the best of people because they would want you to, but don't expect them to be anybody but themselves.

I have one final question. What do people expect of you? In truth, this should not be your concern. Never spend time trying to live up to other peoples' expectations. Always be yourself and refrain from taking the burden of someone else's supposition. When it comes to your personal life, make sure you are fully aware of your loved ones expectations of you. But never let pressure from anyone make you act differently to who you are.

The Importance Of Having Faith

'Faith is one power against which fear cannot stand. Master faith and you will automatically master fear.' **Norman Vincent Peale**

Faith means having confidence and a strong belief in yourself. Even by itself, faith has the power to move our emotional mountains. What an incredible ability to have. Just imagine what you can achieve with it. The good news is that you already have faith. Perhaps though, you may need assistance improving it. For many people, the word 'faith' means religion. In this book, however, I will not be covering that particular interpretation of the word. Rather, I will concentrate on the faith we have in ourselves.

Having faith in yourself and what you are doing is imperative. You need plenty of it for your journey ahead. It is your backup, your silent partner and best buddy. You can only get so far in life without it. In short, faith keeps you going.

Having faith opens up your ability to be persistent. The gift of persistence is one of the major reasons why people succeed in life. Faith, like self-worth can be taken from us but only if we let it happen.

Have faith in yourself, in others and in the world no matter what. It's a better way to live and one that affords greater happiness. Not having faith is a dead end street with a life that leads nowhere. Get ready to assess where you are when it comes to having faith.

Answer the following:

- What do you have faith in?
- Who do you have faith in?

Make a list of all the things in your life that you have faith in. Re-acquaint yourself with faith and remind yourself of how it feels.

Do you have faith in the following?

- Your parents?
- Your siblings?
- Your friends?
- Your partner?
- Your children?
- Your boss?
- Your community?
- Your country?
- What makes you have faith in these?
- What makes you lack faith in any of these?

Figure out how you feel about these important areas of your life and why. Finding out why is so important as most of our feelings come from just one explanation. Discovering what that is will help you understand yourself more. Having a clear picture of your intensity and allocation of faith sheds light on how deeply you believe in yourself and others. For example, when it comes to your loved ones, do you have faith in every aspect of their character or just certain parts?

Those close to you will always sense your lack faith in them. The same is true for you too right? For example, you may have faith in your daughter's ability to be a good businesswoman, but not in her skills as a cook. People close to you want you to have faith in them. It is important to them that you love them and have faith in who they are. It is possible to love someone without having complete faith in them, but it can be a pain-filled relationship. Faith like love has to be unconditional.

To get a deeper understanding about faith, answer the following:

- How much faith do you have in yourself?
- How much faith do you want to have in yourself?

Do you have faith in the following?

- The fact that you will achieve everything you want to?

- The fact that you will always do your best?

- The fact that you are a good person?

- The fact that you are valuable?

Please note that these are all 'facts.'

If you have little faith in yourself, you need to explore why that is. What have you been told, or taught to warrant such an opinion? We shall be discussing this more in Stage Five as we look at self-limiting beliefs. Until then, go through your reasons and look at how you can improve the situation. If you know how vital it is to have faith in yourself, you will be more willing to work on it.

Asking For It

Somewhere down the line to adulthood we lose our ability to ask for what we want. This is strange, as we had no problem doing this as kids as I'm sure your mother will confirm! But as adults, asking for help makes us feel embarrassed. For some reason we have attached a sense of selfishness or guilt to asking. Never feel bad about asking for what you want at any time. It's impossible for others to read your mind so start communicating. Do this as effectively as possible because misunderstandings can cause relationship issues. Let me give you an example. Say you want to have a night away from your family to see some friends. Your family needs to know that you love them yet need some time to re-energize. Once they know this they will support you.

No matter what you need to ask for, express yourself in a warm and loving way. Avoid blame or communication breakdowns. Get in the habit of asking for what you want freely and effectively.

There are some basic human desires we all share, like wanting to be loved for example. Such things we cannot ask for. We have to provide them our self. It's the same as the principle we talked about in Stage One, don't expect others to provide you with what you should be providing for yourself.

The Common Pitfalls To Creating Happiness

You now have an insight into the four main elements to creating what you want. Next take a look at the common pitfalls that could prevent you from getting it.

They include:

Self-sabotage	Fear
Good intentions	Resistance

The Truth About Self-Sabotage

Self-sabotage is when we are our own worst enemy. We disrupt the success or happiness we have created, or are trying to create, through subconscious actions that are based on our negative beliefs. The biggest issue is not being aware of our behavior. For example, let's say you have a good job, but feel inadequate. You frequently arrive late and miss important deadlines. What happens is that over time you create a situation where your boss notices you for all the wrong reasons. Your job and career are in jeopardy due to your actions. Subconsciously your feelings of inadequacy have created a situation which falls in line with your beliefs about yourself. In other words, if you believe you are not good enough, your actions will eventually create a situation to prove yourself right. Knowing this, you will probably agree that it's good to be very aware of what you really think about yourself.

Become aware of your deeper feelings before they develop into consequences. Some acts of self-sabotage can be very severe, matching in intensity to our negative feelings. For example, if you don't think you deserve happiness, then you will consistently sabotage any opportunities you have to be happy.

Think about your current situation and past behavior.

- Have you ever sabotaged your own happiness?

- If so, why?

- What negative belief about yourself was behind your actions?

It is not always easy to identify acts of sabotage because they can be very subtle. So subtle in fact, that they can be mistaken for accidents. Mislaying or damaging important documents or forgetting to set your alarm clock are great examples. It's up to you to be aware of what you do and why. Ensure your actions are positive and support what you want.

Resistance Is Futile

What do you resist in life? Usually we resist the very things that we need to embrace. Life has a very strict rule of making us deal with what we are resisting by condemning us to face it over and over again until we do. This is because we are supposed to learn certain lessons in life that are hidden within whatever we are resisting. So if we don't learn the lesson when the opportunity presents itself, we move into a cycle of events that takes us right back to where we started. For example, if you resist being alone, then eventually you will end up alone. Once you *get* what you are supposed to from being alone or any other re-occurring situation, then that cycle will end.

Do you have a re-occurring situation in your life? Dating or attracting the same kind of men is a classic example. Frequently loosing your job or falling out with friends are others. If you are aware of one, what do you think you have to learn from it in order to move on?

In Stage Three, I mentioned that being courageous is important for your happiness. Use your newly enhanced self-awareness and courage to identify what you may be resisting and why. Make a commitment to yourself to acknowledge whatever it is. You don't have to manage it straight away, just acknowledge it. Master the first step, then you can move on to the next.

To manage resistance you simply have to let go and surrender to the lesson you have to learn. These lessons are all essential in helping us reach our potential and true destiny. Be open to learning and never fear life's lessons. They are here to help you and ensure that your life is as full and as exciting as it was meant to be. Lessons also have a order to them. First you have to learn one thing before you can learn another and so on.

Embrace the lessons and always be on the look out for them in all kinds of situations. The following exercise will help you discover what you are resisting and why. Simply fill in the gaps:

I resist being .... because I feel....................

I resist feeling....................because this means I............

I resist accepting that..........because it would result in......

I resist (name of person) because they are...... and that makes me feel....................

I resist saying what I feel because....................................

I resist leaving because it will mean................................

I resist seeing it through because....................................

I resist trying too hard because......................................

I resist having.............because that would mean............

I resist change because..

I resist my needs because I feel......................................

I resist thinking about..............because.......................

Constantly be aware of what you are avoiding. Remember that your inner-self will always guide you. Listen to its messages and act upon them.

Who's Afraid Of The Big Bad Wolf?

Have you ever had a child come up to you and say that they are afraid of monsters? Have you noticed that telling them monsters don't exist doesn't really comfort them? Their imagination doesn't believe you! The best way to stop a child being frightened is to explain that all monsters are here to protect them. The same principle applies to us and our fears. Pretending your fears don't exist will not stop them chasing you. Believe that they, like the monsters, can be useful.

Expose your monsters. Declare what you fear. Is it failure, success or change perhaps? We all fear different things but conquering them is an important part of our journey through life. I urge you to name and shame what you fear. Let your monsters out of the closet. Dare to look them straight in the eye and see how frightening they are when you expose them for what they are, a figment of your imagination.

Our fears can be paralyzing, but present us with the opportunity to overcome them. By doing this we will feel heroic, brave and courageous and have more peace, grace and wisdom. True, facing our fears can be daunting, but it is far worse to never move beyond them.

Answer these questions on fear:

- What do you fear the most about life?
- Do you fear failure?
- Do you fear success?
- Do you fear unworthiness?
- Do you fear greatness?
- Do you fear anyone or any one thing?

Then ask yourself:
- How does fear limit my happiness?
- How can I eliminate this fear?

More often than not, we make our fears out to be far more ferocious than they actually are. After we tackle them, we often wonder what we were afraid of in the first place.

Many of our fears are irrational while others may be hiding a truth. This discovery process may be painful at times, but it's only scary if you give it that power. Use the resources you already have like faith, courage and self-belief to neutralize your fears. Expect to win through.

'Pushing through fear is less frightening than living with the underlying fear that comes from a feeling of helplessness.' **Susan Jeffers**

Good Intentions And The Road To Hell

Good intentions, they say, pave the road to hell. But are good intentions really that bad? Surely they are honorable as long as they result in action? But taking the *right* action depends on the clarity and honesty of your intention. For example, let's say your intention is to write a book, but you never get around to finishing it. Why? What happened to your intention?

The answer is that your intention to write a book was not your only intention. Underneath, a stronger intention may have been to avoid criticism. By not completing the book, you ensure that your work is never criticized. When it comes to your intentions, look out for any underlying negative beliefs or counter-intentions you may have. Both will sabotage your efforts.

Real-Life Story

Cathy was a smart lady who was on her way up in the world. She had a great career in investment banking and was popular among her colleagues. She had been working at the same company for two years and was up for her first promotion. After a discussion with her boss, she was shocked to discover that also up for the same promotion was her good friend and colleague, Craig.

Cathy wanted that promotion and worked hard over the next six weeks. She became excited about the possibility of getting it. However, what happened next was a series of disasters for Cathy. Among other things, she lost important reports and client data. This was not like her and so Cathy came to me concerned about her recent performance and disillusioned about her chances of getting promoted. She was only four weeks away from decision time and wanted to know what to do to salvage the situation.

The Coach Approach

The first question I asked Cathy was what achieving her intention of winning (her word) the promotion would actually mean to her. She spent some time telling me about all the benefits the promotion would bring her and how it would help her career. Then, I asked her would getting the promotion cost her anything? She fell silent for the longest time. Suddenly she realized how she had viewed the promotion. Because Craig was in the running too, she had seen it as a competition between them. I then asked her what would happen if she did indeed 'win' the competition and get the promotion. Quietly she said, 'If I won then Craig would have to lose.'

'And what else?' I said. Cathy replied, 'I like Craig too much for him to lose!'

Bingo! Cathy had a revelation. She discovered that her intention on the surface was to get the promotion, but her stronger or true intention was not to upset a friend. The effect of her underlying intention made Cathy unconsciously sabotage her chances of getting the promotion. Unbelievable? In my experience your strongest intention is that powerful.

The Result

Cathy and I worked on the power of intentions and her beliefs behind them. She now understands that no one has to suffer because of her success. She reframed her thoughts about the promotion so that they didn't include winning versus losing, but saw the promotion as a well-earned and guilt-free event. She began to understand that she was not responsible for Craig's, or anyone else's success. Now she believed she was deserving of a promotion without any negative connotations. Cathy soon got back on track and the decision was made in her favor. Now, she uses the power of true intent at home as well as at work.

We sometimes get frustrated with life if things don't happen the way we intend them to. Perhaps this is due to a stronger subconscious intention standing in our way. Deep-rooted intentions can be with us for many years creating behavioral patterns that sabotage our progress. Some years ago, I saw a great team exercise on intentions devised by Brain Klemmer (see the resources section at the back of this book). I want to share this with you because of the amazing insights that it produces. I use this same exercise when coaching teams.

This is how it works: the team is asked to stand up and move to one side of the room. They are then asked who would like to volunteer. This causes a few moments of discomfort until someone steps forward or is pushed. This first simple step reveals a lot about the team.

Next, I get the volunteer to walk from one side of the room to the other in a unique and interesting way. They usually skip or bunny-hop. Then I ask for another person to do the same thing but tell them that no two people are allowed to cross the room in the same way. No copy-cats allowed. After about ten or twelve people have danced, wriggled or slid across the room I stop the exercise. Then I ask the team questions about the exercise and their intentions during it.

I ask the first volunteer: Are you always the first to volunteer? And if they were actually pushed forward instead of volunteering, I ask them if they always let people get away with pushing them in life. Then I turn to the person who pushed them and ask whether they make a habit of pushing people ahead of them? Next I ask the rest of the group why they didn't volunteer to be first. Do they make a habit of hiding or letting others go first? Or did they try to volunteer but were not quick enough? If so, how often does that happen to them in life?

Then I ask the team for their feedback about the exercise. Some team members say that they were waiting for the exercise to stop so that they wouldn't need to go across the room, while others couldn't wait to show off their unique method of room crossing! Some confess that they wanted to go last so they could see what everyone else did first. Some say they couldn't get to the front of the line to cross the room because of the others in their way. It's fascinating stuff.

Once the team has thought about how they acted and why, I ask them, 'How often is the way you acted today the way you normally approach life?' I usually get a thoughtful silence at this point as 'aha!' moments are pinging off all over the place.

Imagine doing this exercise yourself. Would you be the first person to volunteer, or would you hide at the back? What unique way would you use to go cross the room?

What this exercise confirms is that our actions are dictated by our strongest intention. Once you have realized what that is, you can change it. Is your intention to show off stronger than your intention not to embarrass yourself? Or is your intention to be one of the crowd stronger than your intention to get ahead at work?

Another example of good intentions are New Year resolutions. We begin the year full of verve and determination to lose weight, stop drinking, or be a nicer neighbor, but our good intentions quickly dissolve as we slip back into old routines. This happens year after year until we get bored with the concept or begin to believe that resolutions just don't work, whichever comes first. Either way we fail to make the improvements to our lives that we intended. The truth behind our annual resolution flop lies in the fact that we have a stronger counter-intention. Your stronger intention will always win, so make sure you know what it is. Self-awareness and honesty can help you do that. Get to the truth of the matter and then set goals to reach your true intention without any disruptions or disappointments.

The Power Of Choice

The power of choice is a very important gift we give to ourselves. It is about taking control and knowing that you *always* have a choice in any situation. Making choices creates our reality both now and in the future. Every time you make a decision you are adding to, or taking away from, the quality of your life. We can choose whether we want to be a doctor or not, the same way we can choose whether to be a nice person or not. The gift of choice is at its most powerful when we use it positively in negative circumstances. For example, you can choose not to steal even though you have no money for food. Similarly, you can choose whether to forgive someone or seek revenge.

It's time to put your decision-making process under the microscope and check your awareness skills. Answer the following questions in your journal:

- What choices have you made through fear?
- How have these decisions affected your life?
- What do you choose to be and why?
- Is it the best choice for you?
- What choices don't you have in life and why?
- What decisions are made for you and why?
- How does this affect your life?
- What is the best choice you have ever made?
- What is the worst?

Choose to make good choices. Choose love. Choose the best in life. In every situation, what we choose determines the outcome. What you choose today will become part of your history. Therefore, always endeavor to make the best decision you can, especially in challenging situations. Be aware of *how* you make decisions. Because each choice you make has a big impact on your life. Choose with wisdom, courage and love. Never let fear dictate your choices. Be in charge of them and ensure that every one supports you and your happiness.

Having Confidence In Trust

Most of us understand the value of trust. Trust in our family, loved ones, professionals and governments play a big part in our stability as a developed society. We love to trust. Being able to rely on something or someone is a great comfort to us. If we are let down we feel anger, hurt and confusion. Should we experience this once too often we loose our ability to trust anyone. Loosing this ability makes us question our own judgment skills and we therefore lose trust in ourselves. Soon this leads to only trusting the things we know or are familiar. Eventually we never allow ourselves to trust anything new or different.

Trust is similar to faith. It is vital. Moreover, we need to trust ourselves first and foremost. Answer these questions about trust:

- What do you trust in life?
- Who do you trust?
- How well do you trust yourself?
- What simple thing can you do today to improve this?
- How will doing this improve your life?

Think of all the times you have trusted yourself:
- Do you feel you have ever been wrong to do so?
- If so, why?
- How can you create an unshakeable trust system with yourself from now on?

Trust your inner-self and know how to distinguish it from your ego.

Review of Stage Four

You have covered a great deal in this stage and have worked hard. Review what you have gleaned from life and yourself from the main areas we have discussed in this part of The Happiness System.

Before you start the next section and subsequent stages, answer the following questions with as much detail as possible:

1. What did you learn about your own personal power?

    Include;
    1. What was good
    2. What was a surprise
    3. What can be improved.

Now increase your power to trust yourself by completing the following:

    1. What do I trust about myself?
    2. What do I know I can do?
    3. What do I trust about my future?
    4. What part of me do I trust to help me achieve what I want?

PART TWO

THE HEART OF HAPPINESS

Introduction

Many things have been written about happiness in the last two centuries. Some urge us to take the spiritual path and love God while others urge us to just live in the moment. Each has their place in the world. Here though, I will take you through what I consider to be at the heart of happiness. In the next three stages of this book you shall embark upon a journey that will take you to the very essence of true happiness. It's a journey to the center of yourself.

In Part One, you discovered that the truth behind happiness is the truth behind you. This book has not been without its challenges and I congratulate you for coming this far. Now it's time for you to get acquainted with what lies at the heart of real happiness. Fundamentally it is knowing that the time to be your most beautiful is yet to come. If you thought Part One went deep, then brace yourself for a little more intensity. Trust that what you are about to discover is what you are meant to know. Much of the work involved in this section is either about getting rid of what you don't need or building up more of what you do.

For possibly the first time in your life you will be able to take a look into your future with your eyes and heart wide open. It is here that you will understand and absorb the limitless possibilities available to you and your destiny. This next part of your journey will hold yet more challenges, but it will also present you with great rewards to last a lifetime.

In Part Two you will actually start creating happiness step by step. Get ready for some more surprises and life changing exercises to assist you in your final part of The Happiness System.

Stage Five

Make Way For Happiness

'More than ever before, this world needs you and the sacred gifts you hold. All you need is the willingness to do the inner work and bring the light into the darkness' **Debbie Ford**

In this fifth stage you will learn the following:

- How to eliminate your negative beliefs
- How to clear out the clutter in your life
- How to get organized
- How to eliminate frustrations & establish personal boundaries
- How to empower yourself through words
- How to stop blaming & start forgiving
- How to create enormous amounts of love

In this fifth stage, we will make way for happiness. In order for happiness to be created you must first make room for it. First, take a moment to think about how far you have come already. Think about what you have learned from this book. Now think about how much further you can go from here. There is another level to true happiness that goes beyond self-awareness to a state of mind conducive to unconditional love. This is where we are headed. Within this stage lies the most important part of your re-education. Self-love. In learning how to love yourself unconditionally, the true heart of happiness, expect to change your whole approach to life. You will learn some of the most profound philosophies and processes to personal excellence. Be prepared to invest your time and energy as we go through these essential exercises. Keep an open mind and faith in your heart with the knowledge that your life is about to change for the better.

You are also going to create your life's mission and personal legacy. Before we do this, you need to take a little time to clear up one or two things. First we will look at your negative beliefs. Is it time to do some mental spring cleaning? Only when your mind and environment is clear of clutter can you really start creating happiness. This is because you need a firm personal foundation to work from that has no self-imposed limitations. Enjoy this cleansing part of your journey!

How To Eliminate Your Negative Beliefs

Your beliefs are the foundation upon which your life is built. Your beliefs are your philosophy, viewpoint and attitude to life. It is normal for us to listen, observe and copy others. This is why many of your beliefs have been adopted from, or influenced by, other people. But without using your better judgment, you can allow adopted negative beliefs to hold a certain amount of power over what you do. Deep within our psyche we often harbor these limiting beliefs which create re-occurring destructive patterns in our lives that keep us from being truly happy.

In Stage Two, we looked at some of the negative beliefs about happiness and how to dispel them. Now, we will uncover any remaining negative beliefs you may have and replace them with more positive ones. This process may seem a little daunting, especially if you already know what your negative beliefs are. But don't allow fear to get in the way of your progress.

Truth And Consequences
Imagine you hold the belief that you can never have the job you truly want. Unless this negative belief is dealt with, you will always struggle with your career. Every time you go for a new job, or get a new job, you will be carrying this belief around with you. Eventually it will manifest itself in a self-sabotaging situation to prove you right.

Henry Ford once said:

*'If you think you **can** do a thing, or think you **can't** do a thing, you're right!'*

There are so many people in history who have done outstanding things because they had the unwavering belief that they could achieve it. Is it time for you to adopt a more positive mindset?

Take your journal. For this seven-step exercise, you need to think clearly so sit somewhere where you won't be disturbed.

1. Write a list of all the negative or limiting beliefs you have about yourself, the world, friends and family. Write what is authentic to you.

2. Many of our limiting beliefs are adopted from the people of influence in our lives. Mark clearly which beliefs on your list are genuinely yours and which may have come from someone else.

3. Next, write an explanation alongside each one explaining where it came from and what evidence you have to prove that it's right.

4. Write down what you think has to change, or what you have to do, in order for you to stop believing it.
   Bear in mind that we harbor negative beliefs about ourselves even though we may have proven them wrong in the past. We only remain mentally bound to them because of low self-esteem.

5. Take each belief in turn and start building a case against it. Do this by going into your past. Collect all the examples you can of when you proved them to be a lie. There *will* be examples, so think hard.

6. Go through your entire list repeating the process until you have built enough evidence to wipe out each one.

7. To make sure that a negative belief doesn't sneak back, replace it with a positive one.

Here's an example:

Negative belief:
I don't believe I am good enough to get a promotion.

Explanation:
I believe this because there must be better qualified candidates.

Evidence to dispel the belief:
I am liked and respected among my colleagues. My boss understands my ambition within the company. I have been promoted before. I have had good reviews. I am worthy of it. I will be a good addition to the team as I have been in others.

Replacing the belief:
I know I am good enough to be considered for the promotion. From now on, I will endeavor to learn as much as I can about my potential new role and what I need to do to secure the promotion I know I deserve.

When you use this system for discounting your negative beliefs, be totally honest with yourself. Don't write something you think is right, make sure it is really true for you. Also, be honest about how good you really are. This is more difficult than you first imagine! But get comfortable with self-praise.

Stubborn Beliefs

Take a look at your list. Are there any negative beliefs that are impossible to extinguish? If so, ask yourself the following:

1. How does believing this benefit me?
2. What would be the worst that could happen if I believed this for the rest of my life?
3. What is stopping me from letting go of it?
4. What would I rather believe?
5. What would be the worst that could happen if I believed this for the rest of my life?

Now you have more reasons to dispel the belief. Building emotional reasons instead of logical ones is more powerful and effective for demolishing your limiting thoughts.

Affirmations

If a negative belief proves to be rather stubborn to get rid of then re-write it in a positive way in the future tense. In other words, turn it into an affirmation. For example, if you believe that you are not good at selling, write an affirmation like; 'I am increasing my power to sell every day.'

Make a copy of your affirmation and stick it where you have plenty of opportunities to see it, like your bathroom mirror for example. This will be a physical reminder of your potential and that your past results do not equal your future ones. Eventually, the affirmation will become so familiar to your subconscious that your brain will get busy finding ways to make it a physical reality. This is a simple example of how powerful your thoughts are. Be aware that affirmations should be positive, truthful and only require your trust in them to make them transpire.

How To Clear Out The Clutter In Your Life

Now that you have learned to get rid of negative beliefs, the next stage is to eliminate all your other trash. From your environment to your personal life, you are about to do some major spring-cleaning! Trash is stuff you have accumulated over the years and is surplus to your requirements. All the stuff that is no longer useful to you or past its sell-by-date has to go! One person can create a surprising amount of physical garbage in a short space of time. Sometimes, we only get around to clearing it out when we actually move home. Then there are some who just take it with them!

People also collect a great deal of mental trash too, like bad relationship habits. We shall take a look at some examples of mental trash to see how you can rid yourself of it for good. This simple process of 'out with the old and in with the new,' eradicates staleness, dead wood and pure junk that has been hanging around and clogging up your life. You need to make room for newer, fresher things. The Law of Physics states that no two things can occupy the same space at the same time. So according to this simple scientific rule you have to throw out all those things in your life that no longer serve you to make room for ones that can. Give yourself a fresh start to create a happier environment all round for you and your family. You will be amazed at how quickly this works.

Physical Environment
Over the next two months, go through your home room by room. Clear out all the stuff you don't use. There may be some things you would like to keep for sentimental reasons, but be strict. Don't hold on to anything that doesn't have some sort of value in your life. Clothes and shoes collecting dust in your closet have to go. Send them to a charity. Look for items you never wear. Keep what you wear 80% of the time and give the rest away. Chances are, if you haven't worn it in the last twelve months then you will never wear it again. Do this for your summer and winter clothes and give away what you don't want.

Re-invigorate your home by freeing it from unwanted clutter. Clear out broken or never used objects, hardware and other paraphernalia. You never know what you might find hidden under the clutter! I know many people who have done this and made extra cash selling their unwanted items at a garage sale.

Having a big clear out will make you feel more relaxed and less stressed about your environment. When you have a little less chaos in your life, you can see things more clearly and feel more energetic. Once you have spring-cleaned, keep a tight control over what you allow in to your home. Be vigilant with your shopping and storing and be determined to keep your home tidy. Your state of mind is reflected directly in the state of your environment. Help your state of mind by keeping your environment free of trash.

Relationship Rubbish

Some things are a little harder to throw out, like relationships for example. But it is essential to your happiness that you rid your life of the relationships that no longer work. Our relationships have a profound effect on our emotional wellbeing and as women we have a variety of complicated relationships to handle. Take this opportunity to contemplate each relationship you have in your life like family, friends, work colleagues and associates. Some of these relationships will need refining and re-defining. Some may need a lot more work to justify their existence. Also there are those that expired a long time ago and are holding you back.

Get out your broom. Make sure it is a big one because these old relationship cobwebs aren't always easy to sweep away. It takes a lot of guts to make a clean sweep. But I will help you do what you need to do through this next exercise.

Take your journal and write down your answers to the following:

- Who in my life is no longer healthy for me?
- Who or what am I clinging on to and why?
- What kind of relationship do I have with those closest to me?
- Are they as good as I want them to be?
- How do I want to improve them?

Parents and other family relationships can nearly always be improved if the will is there. However, fair-weather friends and old flames are the worst culprits for out-of-date relationships. These require your attention first. Do not be afraid to draw any unhealthy relationship to a close. Believe that a better relationship is waiting to come into your life when you have created the necessary space for it.

A guideline for picking out the not-so-good relationships is to make sure that everyone in your life loves you just the way you are. Be sure they are there for you and give back just as much love and support as you give them. Anyone who fails this assessment is not worthy of your time. If you feel anxious about ending a relationship, think about what you gain by keeping it in your life. A fear of not being able to replace it usually prevents us from letting go. Always do what is best for you taking guidance from your inner-self.

Now let's take a look at how you can improve those relationships you wish to keep. You're aware that you can never change someone right? Instead we will look at how you can make small and simple adjustments to make things better almost instantly.

First we shall focus on your family. You love them yet they can drive you crazy! What's new?! The core of making the most of your family relationships is to accept and love them despite their foibles. Tell them that you love them. Forgive them silently for being annoying and spend as much time with them as you can.

Sometimes, being around our families can make it difficult for us to grow. They can often see us as we were, not as we are. You will always be someone's little girl or younger sister, but don't let their outdated outlook stop you from developing your relationship with them. Communicate lovingly and with patience. Don't make demands or blame them for any past misery. Start fresh and learn to love them as individuals understanding that they too are struggling with issues and limiting beliefs. It's not your job to change or save them. But it is your choice as to whether you make moves to improve your relationship or not.

Next let's discuss the relationships of the heart. Yes, your love life. Oh how women struggle! We see romantic love as the most central thing in our lives. Women look for their soul-mate, that perfect love. This search has become the topic that launched thousands of magazine articles, TV programmes and movies. What is the secret to finding the man of your dreams? Well, it's simple.

The 11 Point Guide to Healthy Relationships of the Heart:

1. Know yourself first
2. Don't bring any baggage from past relationships
3. Don't have poor expectations
4. Don't have unrealistic expectations
5. Give as well as take
6. Communicate your feelings with love and respect
7. Don't expect to be healed or saved
8. Know what you want from a partner
9. Know what you have to offer them
10. Don't feel or act desperately
11. Know that the greatest love affair you will ever have is the one you have with yourself

Again let me emphasize that above romantic love, is the love you have for yourself. It is your most important relationship. Make sure it is free from negativity and limits. Loving yourself first ensures that you enjoy all the other relationships in your life. Having a healthy relationship with yourself is absolutely vital.

In relationships with others, never tolerate those who harm you. At the same time be willing to forgive. Always make the first move to rise above silly tensions or misunderstandings. If others fail to respond to your efforts, accept it, forgive them and move on. (There is more detail about self-love and forgiveness later on in this book.)

Polishing Up Your Act

Do you have any naughty habits? You know the kind of habit that is not good for you, but you do it anyway? If so, it's time to replace it with a healthier one. After all, it's impossible to be the best you can be with a cigarette hanging out of your mouth! Bad habits are not cool!

Can you claim any of the following bad habits?

Unhealthy eating
Smoking
Not getting enough sleep
Getting too much sleep
Taking little or no exercise
Always being late
Not keeping in contact with old friends

These are just some of the bad habits we adopt in life. Expose yours now. Did you know that your top five habits predict your future? It's true! Write down your bad habits including those you only do now and again. The lesson here is to replace them with healthier ones, just like you did with your negative beliefs. Polishing up your act means making sure you only care for what truly matters in life like love, family and friendship. You don't waste time on destructive habits like gossiping; instead you reside on a higher level of awareness.

Ensure that everything that you do from now on adds to your life and to the lives of others. Clear out energy drainers like negative thoughts, actions, relationships and habits for good. Instead, do things that give you energy and make you feel good. Compile a list of what gives you energy. Ask yourself; what makes me feel good?

How To Get Organized

Enjoy a better quality of life by becoming more organized. The benefits of good time-management and planning exceed efficiency. Being organized means you can accomplish more in less time, never forget an important event and no longer have to rush around like a fool on wheels. Being organized gives you the precious gift of time and self-confidence. Having more time means you arrive relaxed and feeling great. It also means you have more time to be with your family and friends. Taking time out to make more time makes all the difference. It's easier than you think.

Take five minutes, that's all, at the end of each day to plan the next. Better still, take five minutes on a Sunday evening to plan the week ahead. Or go wild and plan months ahead! Planning helps create more balance in your life. You are less frantic and more capable when you know what's going on. After all, there is everything to gain from having an organized life but only a stomach ulcer to gain from living in pandemonium. A little time spent thinking ahead saves you oodles of extra time each day. To start with, what activities can you reject to give you back more time?

Some people are disorganized for a reason. To them creating a commotion subconsciously supports a negative belief they have about themselves. For example; if a woman thinks she is a bad mother, she will make parenting chaotic and dramatic to feel that she is right.

Think carefully about how you organize your life. If chaos tends to rule, look at why that is. Is it hiding something else? Remember that there is nothing to fear, so don't let anything hold you back from getting to the bottom of the issue. Indeed, there may not be an issue at all, but the sooner you check, the sooner you can create more happiness.

The reverse can also be true. Some people are too organized. They only feel happy when everything is in its right place. Being tidy and on top of things is great, but letting it take over your life is a sign of a deeper issue.

To find out where you are when it comes to being organized answer the following:

- What areas of your life could do with a little more organization?
- What would be the main benefit of this?
- What part of your daily routine is the hardest to get right?
- What part of your day do you enjoy the most?
- What can you do today to increase the time you spend doing that?
- What can you let go of in life?
- How will you benefit from doing this?

It isn't necessary to make huge changes in your daily routine to benefit from being organized. Take one area at a time and see the changes happen more quickly than you would expect.

Being organized and prepared is an excellent habit to have. It makes life easier for all concerned, and let's face it, we always admire those who appear organized. It is not that difficult to make improvements no matter how crazy your schedule is. A little can go a long way and make a world of difference to your life. Adopt a new habit today. Organize your life a little more so you can spend time doing the things you want to.

How To Eliminate Frustrations & Establish Your Boundaries

Two fundamentals of creating happiness are having little to endure and having well-established personal boundaries. Put simply, nothing in your life irritates you. You have managed to eliminate every one of your frustrations and your personal boundaries are being constantly honored. Perhaps this seems too idealistic? Not so. It is up to you how you choose to look at it. You alone decide what you tolerate or not. Either way, you are the only one who can make the difference. Both eliminating your frustrations and personal boundary building are essential for creating happiness.

Not having well-established boundaries in your relationships can lead to a lot of unhappiness. Establishing and communicating your boundaries will determine how people treat you. It is up to you to teach people what is acceptable to you and what is not. Ensure you are respected. Be a confident person who knows who they are and what they want. Those who love you will always honor your boundaries. Others may need a little training! You have to believe it is right to set standards. Communicate them carefully but firmly. Set personal boundaries and always keep them in order to honor yourself.

Frustrations

Tolerating offensive people or uncomfortable situations may sometimes seem the easier option. But creating happiness requires you to work a little harder. Think about what you are tolerating in life right now. Write a list in your journal of all the people or situations that frustrate you. Start by asking yourself the following questions:

What am I tolerating...
- at work?
- at home?

- within my family?
- with friends?
- in my intimate relationships?
- during my leisure time?
- in my immediate environment?
- within myself?

Then for each of your answers ask yourself:

- Why do I choose to tolerate it?
- What would happen if I chose not to tolerate it any more?
- What would continue to happen if I did?
- What would my life be like if I had nothing to tolerate?

By completing this exercise you will begin to see beyond your frustrations as you visualize your life without them. Creating this compelling vision of your future gives you the added strength and determination to rid your life of any suffering. Remember, there is nothing to fear. If you feel apprehensive about eliminating any of your frustrations, think about how this will compromise your life both now and in the future.

Now you have a good idea of what you are tolerating and what life would be like without them. The next step is to go ahead and eliminate them. Each frustration is different but most can be worked on by using your self-coaching powers. For example, let's say you were frustrated about your mother-in-law's attitude towards you. You will never change her behavior (unless you have a miracle up your sleeve), but as she is a part of your life, how can you make the best out of this potentially painful situation? As a coach I may not have miracles up my sleeve, but I do have a few tricks! In this instance I would like to introduce you to my power tool called 'reframing.' In situations like the one I have just described, where the sense of hopelessness is evident - simply reframe it.

This trick can give you a fresh perspective and a sense of renewed possibility in the most frustrating circumstances. Instead of focusing on what's irritating you, put your energy into seeing it more positively. Take the case of the mother-in-law from hell; reframe her appalling behavior from something to take personally, to her way of showing you her limitations. Rather than rejoice in the fact that she has limitations, approach your encounters with her with more compassion. Now you have changed the theme from *my mother-in-law is out to get me*, to *I am a compassionate and patient person*. Reframe your frustrations so you see them more positively and less personally.

Personal Boundaries

Your personal boundaries are what you decide is ok and what is not. For example, one of your personal boundaries may be 'no one can shout at me.' Or another could be 'I only work with people who are passionate about what they do.' Your personal boundaries are the standards you live by. Therefore, honoring your personal boundaries is vital for your self-esteem. When you respect and love yourself enough to honor each one of your boundaries in any given situation you can welcome an abundance of happiness into your life.

Ask yourself the following:

- What are my personal boundaries?
- Where do I draw the line when it comes to situations and relationships?
- Have my boundaries ever been breached? If so, when?
- How do I approach the situation when this happens?

Respecting your boundaries makes you feel good and creates a positive guideline for every other scenario in your life. As women, I believe we should have very clear boundaries in all our relationships. In coaching, I find the following exercise absolutely crucial for creating happiness and so I have included it for you to try too. Take time to complete the following:

Take your journal and begin by identifying your boundaries. Be honest with yourself. Ask yourself; what are my boundaries when it comes to....

- work?
- home?
- family?
- friends?
- intimate relationships?
- having fun?
- my immediate environment?

You now you have a blueprint for a happier life. Now you have established exactly what your personal boundaries are in all areas of your life, never go back on them. The people worth having in your life are the ones who will always respect your boundaries.

How To Empower Yourself Through Words

The pen is mightier than the sword! I believe the same is also true of the spoken word. Words hold incredible power. Enough power in fact to create or devastate. An idea or suggestion can be destroyed or brought to life by words alone.

Often people use words to hurt others. So imagine then the power our own words have on our life. The words you use greatly influence your reality and destiny. Watching what words you use when you are talking to, or about, yourself is especially important.

For example, using negative words like these:

It's so *stressful*	I can *never* manage to…
It's so *hard*	I am *useless* at that
It's *impossible*	I *can't*

When you do this, you are giving these negative words power over how you think and act. This in turn pre-programs your future.

Replace negative words with more positive ones. For example, replace *difficult* with *challenging*. This instantly changes the situation. How you communicate with yourself influences your perception. If you have described something as difficult, it's just difficult and you have disarmed yourself by making things a struggle. If however, you use the word *challenging* you have added a little excitement and adventure to the situation. I grant you, it is challenging to decide what you are going to say before you say it. It's an art in itself! But once mastered, it creates far more positive experiences.

Think about how you describe your life, or any situation. How many of the following expressions do you use?

- I am always doing that
- I don't think I can
- I am so stressed out
- I am always tired
- I can't understand it
- I am never going to be able to have that
- I am never going to be able to do that
- I am never going to be able to be that
- I don't have the time

Do you see how using these very common expressions can affect your life?

When The Stars Are Aligned In The Right Way, Then I Can Be Happy!

Sound familiar? Perhaps you are guilty of starting a sentence by saying:

'I'll be happy when...........'

Don't wait you whole life for certain things to happen before you will let yourself be happy. To me, throwing obstacles in the way of creating happiness is inventing certain conditions before for it can happen. Is it martyrdom or madness? More often than not, these conditions are ones that we have little or no control over and so the responsibility of our happiness is out of our control. Now we have a perfect excuse for not being happy. Because it is out of our hands, it isn't our fault. Never put conditions on what you want in life. It will make it very challenging to attain them. Have you put any conditions on creating your own happiness?

Be aware of how you use words. Use ones that work for you and not against you. Start practicing today. See how you can immediately improve a situation purely by how you use words.

Passing The Buck

Blaming others is shedding responsibility for your own actions. When we are blaming others, we use phrases like; *she made me do it* or *you made me feel bad*. The truth is no one makes us *do* or *feel* something unless we let them. Blaming others makes us powerless. Deep down we know that it is not right but we say it just to cop out. Others do the same to us for the exact same reason.

How To Stop Blaming & Start Forgiving

Being able to forgive is perhaps one of the most powerful acts a human can perform. Not only does it stop us from holding other people responsible for our circumstances in life, it allows us to grow. Gandhi once said: 'The weak can never forgive. Forgiveness is the attribute of the strong.' And he was right. Harnessing such a power, instead of holding grudges or seeking revenge, is the quicker route to happiness. You are freeing your life from pain by being able to forgive those who have harmed you. Once you have forgiven someone, the pain quickly subsides because you have let go of anger and resentment. Beat the temptation to feel bitter. If you can reach beyond it, you can find peace and tranquility. No matter what others do to you, you have the power to forgive them.

Some people are wary of forgiving. They belief forgiving gives someone permission to offend again. So not forgiving them is their assurance that it won't. This is punishing behavior for all concerned. It is living in fear of another person's power. In these circumstances, forgiveness is the only way to regain power and take back control.

The act of forgiveness can make you feel incredibly good. The sense of doing what is right is a heartfelt one. Also, by forgiving someone you no longer have to worry about the situation, it has been resolved. Forgive those in your past and present for their actions. Free yourself to face your future with a clean slate.

In your life, who is waiting to be forgiven?

Real-Life Story

Jean came to me because she wanted more peace and relaxation. She felt held back in life due to her important responsibilities. Her children were in college, but most of her time was spent looking after her elderly widowed mother. Her mother Irene lived in a small apartment behind Jean's house and relied on her daughter to do everything for her. Jean was Irene's only child and so felt duty bound to care for her. But caring for Irene was making Jean emotionally exhausted. Jean's husband worked long hours so was unable to help her which caused a lot of friction between them. Jean had thought about hiring a professional nurse but Irene refused to co-operate. Subsequently, Jean started to feel resentment towards her mother as she began to feel trapped.

The Coach Approach

I asked Jean what one small thing could make this situation better, but she was adamant that the situation was impossible. Then I asked her to write down all the different aspects of the situation that frustrated her. Needless to say Jean wrote a long list. I asked her to go through each frustration with me, explaining each one in turn. Her list included both practical and emotional issues.

I asked Jean to focus on her practical frustrations first. As she went through them we discussed ways to overcome them. We brainstormed ideas that would result in less work for her. Next we turned our attention to her emotional frustrations. I asked Jean to separate her list into three categories. The first one was for the frustrations she had that centered on herself. The next was for her frustrations about her mother and the last one was for her husband-related ones.

She looked at her husband's list first. I asked her how she could resolve these frustrations immediately without asking him to do anything. Jean thought long and hard and soon began to realize that the first thing she could do in order to move on would be to forgive her husband. She started by forgiving him for having to work so hard and for always being tired at the end of each day. She also forgave him for not really understanding how she felt. Immediately after doing this Jean started to feel a lot better.

Feeling empowered, she then moved on to her list about her mother. Once again Jean realized that the only way to become unstuck in this situation would be to forgive her mother too. She began by forgiving her for refusing any outside assistance and for needing so much care and so on. Jean now began to feel enormous amounts of relief. Finally, she came to her own list. She never realized how much she had blamed herself for her circumstances. She realized she had to forgive herself too for not being a better daughter, wife or nurse.

The Result

Jean learned that in difficult situations, one of the first things to do is to start forgiving. When you start to forgive, much of the anguish in a situation disappears. You start to see things more clearly. Jean could have chosen to feel resentment for many *years but it would not have changed the situation. Immediate improvements can be made when we decide to forgive.*

With this new perspective, Jean's whole perspective changed. She began to treasure the time she had left with her mother and made an effort to make caring for her as fun as possible. Her relationship with her husband changed for the better too. She no longer complained to him about her mother, instead she told him about their day together. Jean found the peace she was looking for. It was just surprising to her how it came about.

I Forgive Me

Forgiveness should always include you too. You should always forgive yourself for what you feel you have done wrong. We all make mistakes or do things we are not proud of so don't punish yourself, forgive yourself. By forgiving, you have the power to see your mistakes for what they were, learning opportunities!

This exercise is very important. Take time to do this thoroughly and clear the way to a more forgiving future. Go right back into your past and dig out all the things you still haven't forgiven yourself for and fill in the blanks:

I forgive myself for thinking that.......................

I forgive myself for believing that......................

I forgive myself for saying that..........................

I forgive myself for doing................................

I forgive myself for being................................

I forgive myself for having...............................

I forgive myself for not thinking that.......................

I forgive myself for not believing that........................

I forgive myself for not saying...........................

I forgive myself for not doing..................................

I forgive myself for not being..................................

I forgive myself for not having................................

Always forgive yourself. It leaves you open for developing into a more loving person. You can only truly love yourself when you have no bad feelings about yourself. Forgiveness clears the way for you to be happy. Forgiveness, like most things in life, is a choice. Choose to forgive and see how different your outlook on life becomes. Actively forgive all the time. Do not pre-condition forgiveness, just forgive because you can. It is self-healing and an act of self-love.

How To Create Enormous Amounts Of Love

Self-love, as you may have guessed by now, is the running theme in this book. This is because as women, we judge ourselves against an image we have of perfection and analyze ourselves for not living up to this ideal. In short, we reject ourselves. Then we look to others to love us instead. Feeling the need for another person's love to make us feel worthy is a tragedy. Often we don't realize we are perfect just as we are.

Don't spend your life on a love diet. Feeling needy, desperate or starving yourself of love will make you jump from one relationship to another. Next will come the dreaded questions: What did I do to deserve this pain? Will I ever find love again?'

The truth is, we are sometimes afraid to love. We fear the pain of rejection and so the simple answer to this is to love yourself first. Don't reject this idea because you have been taught that self-love is vanity. This is a myth. When a woman truly loves herself, she is not arrogant or shallow, she is peaceful and confident. There is nothing negative about loving yourself. It gives you great strength and above all, it gives you the ability to love others.

Truly loving someone is not asking for anything. It is just being happy that they are alive. The same is true for loving yourself. There should be no conditions attached. As women, we often have huge conditions to self-love. We use 'if only' expressions. See if you are one such lady. Own up if you have used any of the following phrases:

'If only I were…

taller	smarter	prettier
shorter	funnier	more confident
thinner	bigger breasted	less like me
stronger	quieter	more like her

Love yourself. You are who you are, and that alone is amazing. Self-love is not about being selfish, but about being self-full. You are complete. You no longer need to search for what you *should* be. Enjoy being you. When you love yourself unconditionally, you no longer worry about your looks, age, being single, being divorced or being right. You believe you are perfect despite your flaws!

Remember, the love you want in life can only come from you. Everything else is a bonus. The degree to which you love yourself is the degree to which you will be happy.

Know What's True

Loving yourself starts with the truth. You have to stop pretending everything in your life is ok if it is not. Self-loathing is a common trait. It can lead to many different forms of self-abuse and neglect. Embracing the truth about yourself and seeing yourself as you really are sets you free. As a woman, you must master self-acceptance. These questions are designed to get you to think deeply about how you feel and act towards yourself. Think about your answers carefully. As always, be honest.

Answer the following questions:

- How much do you love yourself?

- What conditions do you put on loving yourself?

- What is stopping you from loving yourself more?

- What do you like about yourself?

- What do you dislike?

- Have you forgiven yourself for it yet?

- Do you communicate lovingly with yourself?

- Do you spend time alone?

- If not, why?

- How can you increase your feelings of self-love right now?

Start to use your powers of courage and forgiveness to help you improve your feelings of self-love.

Self-love is the journey of a lifetime, your one great mission. Help yourself to love yourself more through simple things like gifting yourself more time to do what you love doing. Teach yourself how to give and receive love more readily by understanding that you can never have too much love in your life. Begin loving from within because *you* are at the heart of happiness.

Review of Stage Five

Wow! You have done so well. Take a look at how far you have come. Congratulate yourself! You are making wonderful progress through The Happiness System and are very close to completing it.

These questions should help you confirm what you have just learned and take you on a few steps further. Take a few moments to consider the following:

1. How do you feel now that you have faced and conquered your negative beliefs and eliminated your frustrations?

2. Do you feel you want to do more work on any of the exercises found in this stage? If so, which ones?

3. Review any of the exercises in any of these stages.

Before you move on to the next stage, do you have any negative feelings or emotions about your life? If so, what exercise can you use to eliminate them?

Stage Six

Creating True Happiness

'I know for sure that I created this happiness by choice. And I know it's really not just one choice that matters-it's all the baby choices that will lead you to the ultimate moment, when you can make the strongest stand and commitment to yourself and the life that's calling your name.' **Oprah**

In this sixth stage you will learn the following:

- How to change your perspective to change your life
- How to live gracefully
- How to honor your values
- How to make you wishes come true
- How to use your body to create happiness
- How to eliminate problems

By coming this far, you will have a far better understanding than most about how happiness is created. The question is, now that you have this information, what are you going to do with it? Well I have ensured that Stage Six gives you the opportunity to use what you have learned. Now you can discover more about yourself than you ever thought possible.

I am going to take you through several steps of life mastery. Mastery of course takes practice. But as you develop more and increase your emotional intelligence, your whole perspective on life will change too. All remaining happiness obstacles and limitations are about to be wiped out so you can continue on your journey more dynamically and successfully.

You have shown an incredible commitment to yourself by working through so much of this system. Take advantage of the momentum you have created by learning how you fortify your development through enthusiasm.

How To Change Your Perspective To Change Your Life

Your perspective is your outlook on life. So is your wine glass half full or half empty? Life has its ups and its downs so being upbeat all the time is far from easy. If we let them, our down times can take over and our sunny smile becomes a grimace. One way to prevent the blues becoming your new color scheme is to embrace enthusiasm. Now being enthusiastic is not always in vogue. Indeed in some circumstances it is highly inappropriate. But you cannot argue the fact that enthusiasm in a person can light up a room.

Most of us just simmer away, lukewarm never really living life to the full. Truly being alive is to bubble, boil and burst with joy. Enthusiasm is the essence to a joyous life. The energy you create has the power to move mountains and achieve great things. Come to think of it, what is ever accomplished without enthusiasm?

Optimism is the mother of enthusiasm. You have to be optimistic before you can generate enthusiasm. Optimism comes from our beliefs and is therefore a choice. To help you make the right choice you have to understand how being the opposite, i.e. pessimistic will affect your life. Thinking pessimistically is a self-fulfilling prophecy because it creates bad life experiences. You live a second-rate life where you feel burnt out, put out and down and out. It's not pleasant!

No one is born a pessimist. It takes a bit of work. But by a surprisingly young age we acquire the necessary skills and become very good at it. Unlearning such a talent requires us to go back to kindergarten, mentally speaking, to write a very simple list. Here is how it works: write in your journal a list of all your assets – personal assets as opposed to financial ones. Write down as many assets as you can and include your mental, physical and spiritual ones.

Next continue on with your list but this time include general assets or good things about the world including your family, the weather and anything else that comes to mind.

Becoming more optimistic needs a little effort and concentration. You are creating a new habit, a new way of being you. Instead of worrying and stewing over things you overcome doubt, anger, impatience and fear. All your old internal enemies are conquered and life takes on a new brighter look.

Complete the exercise below to give yourself a clear idea of how being positive will affect your life for the better. Use your journal and answer the following questions:

1. On an optimism scale from 1 to 10 (10 being high), what do I score?

2. What does being more optimistic mean to me?

3. How will being more optimistic help me create happiness?

4. How will my life be affected if I am not optimistic?

5. What do I need to change to become more optimistic?

6. How will my family be affected if I am more optimistic?

7. Who can I use as a role model to help me become more optimistic?

8. What do I have to do to score of 10 out of 10 for optimism?

9. What can I do daily to ensure I maintain this score?

10. What will it take for me to score 12 out of 10?

Your Life Metaphorically Speaking

How do you use metaphors? Most of us use them to describe life. For example 'life is a game.' Metaphors reveal a rich and full picture of our mindset in one simple sentence. Earlier, we discussed the importance of using positive words, now I want to explain how this is also true for our use of metaphors.

Metaphors can be as harmful as using negative words or thinking negative thoughts. Ultimately, using the wrong metaphor can work against you. Here are some other examples of the metaphors people use when describing life:

- Life's a struggle
- Life's suffering
- Life's a battle
- Life's a party
- Life's an adventure

You can tell from the above list which metaphors are the more positive ones. One of my favorites is 'life is a play.' This is because using the analogy of a play to me means you decide who is in your play and for how long. I use it in an empowering way. Think of a metaphor for how you view life. Make it positive and fun.

Answer the following:

- What other metaphors do you use in life?
- How do you describe love for example?
- How do they affect your happiness?
- Do they often change?
- Which metaphors can you use to experience life more positively?

The Rules

Having a metaphor for life means you live by certain rules. This is only a good thing when the rules support your values. Check to see what criteria you have for living a good life.

- Do you have high standards?
- Do you play fair in life?
- Which rules do you have in life?
- Do they empower your life?
- Which rules don't?
- Which rules can you adopt now to improve your life?

Other People's Opinions

As women, we love to get other people's opinions. Whether it's for buying a dress or a house, we want to know what others think. For our most important transactions in life, we seek the opinion of those we love and respect. We like to have support, encouragement and time-saving bits of advice. Unlike men, we don't mind asking for assistance! In fact, we value it enormously. We love being asked our opinion nearly as much as we love giving it. It makes us feel important and appreciated. What we need to be careful of though, is relying on other people's opinions when it comes to making choices about our personal life.

Often we ask friends what to do, whether they are qualified to help us or not. Friends may be having problems of their own or may have their own agenda when it comes to our life. We ask our friends and family to guide us because we feel we need their support. There's no harm in listening to their advice, just as long as we use our own judgment when it comes to making decisions. You should always feel free to do what you think is right, no matter what other people say. You are the best judge of what's right for you. Remaining in control and taking full responsibility for the outcomes helps you become more confident and self-reliant.

How To Live Gracefully

How you react to situations determines how happy you are. In other words, it's not the problem itself, but how you react to it that creates the problem. It's about your levels of will and grace when facing tricky situations. Your 'will' is how you choose to react. This directly determines your level of grace (dignity). If you want to live more gracefully you need to control your will.

Think back to a time when you reacted angrily to someone. What was the result of your actions? Usually, a negative reaction will create more negativity. This causes the situation to deteriorate rapidly. I know it is not always easy to control how we react, but there are ways to make improvements. Sometimes we have automatic responses to certain situations so we have to stop and think about these to make sure they are positive.

The first thing to do is to develop a better understanding of how people tick. It's important to know where people are coming from when you are communicating with them. People say or do bad things for a reason. It may not be justifiable, but it's a reason nonetheless. Their behavior is usually serving a need. It's not up to you to work things out for them. All you have to do is see through their actions to the truth. Look beyond their behavior. For example, if someone stabs you in the back at work, it is not because they are a bad person, although we all choose how we act. He or she may feel inadequate and do it to feel better. Think of a time when someone wasn't nice to you. What do you think was behind their actions? Is it likely they were hurting inside? What they were feeling may have manifested itself into poor behavior.

Now you know why people act badly you can take it less personally. You now know it's about *them* not you.

The second thing to do is control your emotions. How you feel about yourself determines how vulnerable you are. The reason why most of us react badly to situations is because we feel exposed. Therefore, having a good sense of who you are will help you feel more confident. You will take less notice of what people say and be less open to accepting other people's issues as your own.

Controlling Your Reactions

The next time you find yourself in a situation where you feel you want to react, stop! Think about what has just been said or done. Ask yourself the following questions:

- What is behind their actions?

- What could they be feeling to do or say such a thing?

- How have I reacted to a similar incident before?

- What feelings were behind my reactions then?

- How do I choose to react now?

- What outcome do I want to create from this scenario?

- How can I take charge of the situation?

Answering these questions is creating a proactive approach to life instead of a reactive one. You are ultimately designing harmonious and, therefore, happier outcomes to tricky situations.

Eventually, after some practice, you will be able to do this automatically. Your positive and compassionate reactions will become second nature to you. Try this out as soon as the opportunity arises. I am sure you will be amazed at how you can defuse a potentially sticky situation while helping the offender to reflect upon his or her actions.

How to Honor Your Values

Are you a woman of substance? What values do you live by? If you can answer that you have the key to happiness. This is because you know the essence of who you are. You know your values and so have a better understanding of yourself. When coaching, I always get my clients to go through their values. Most don't know what they are. This is quite common. The truth is every decision we make is dominated by at least one of our top values. It is this very fact that causes people to suffer unnecessarily. It is vitally important for you to know yours. To know what you are ruled by is having access to your behavioral 'blueprint.'

A major key to happiness is honoring your values in every thing you do. When you honor them, you are being true to yourself. You are following your heart and nurturing your soul. But if you don't know what your values are, you cannot honor them.

Anxiety comes from doing something that goes against your values. Living your life according to your values will create more harmony and fulfillment for you and so knowing what they are and living through them, leads to greater feelings of self-worth, and of course, happiness.

What Is A Value?

Values are qualities like honesty, integrity, valor, creativity, love and commitment. If you can't think of a one, think about the characteristics you admire in other people. These attributes are your values.

Below I have listed just of few values to help you:

Creativity	Adventure	Honesty	Beauty
Truth	Integrity	Self-worth	Compassion
Sincerity	Giving	Determination	Humility
Nurturing	Community	Individualism	Unconditional love

Sometimes we can confuse values with a result. Success, for example is a result. You have to create success, so it's not strictly a value. If you are attracted to success then your values would be: dedication, determination or creativity for example. These are the values which can help you become successful. The same is also true for things like 'financial security.' This is a result, not a value. The value would be 'financial literacy.' This value would eventually create the desired result.

The Adoption Process

As I mentioned before, we adopt values into our lives that we admire in others. Our parents and close family usually introduce us to our first set of values. These may be the only ones we choose to have in life. But for most of us, our values change as we meet other significant role models. By the time we are adults, we have a myriad of values from various influential people and experiences.

This stage of the system gives you the ideal opportunity to review your values. It allows you to see which values no longer work for you and it gives you the opportunity to replace them with new and improved ones.

Is It Good For Me?

Subconsciously we put our values in a specific order. Our most important value is positioned at number one. This value is the most dominant and has the greatest influence over our wellbeing. This is why it is essential not only to be aware of your top values, but also ensure that they support you 100%. Some values may appear inspiring and worthy on the surface, yet may create unfavorable effects. A good example is 'honor.' You may think it is a suitable value to have. It appears to be a noble value but it can be a tough task-master. For example, if honor is your top value, then you will prize it above other values like 'kindness.' Having honor above kindness may not be entirely appropriate for a happy ending in many circumstances.

Another area you have to be aware of when it comes to your values is balance. You should always maintain equilibrium in your top values. To have 'giving' as a value is good, but less so if it is not accompanied with an ability to receive. You need to be able to do both in order to be happy.

Overall, make sure your values are positive ones and support you in every way. Additionally, ensure that your values apply to you first and foremost. For example, if 'loyalty' is a top value for you, make sure that loyalty to yourself comes before loyalty to others. The same applies to other values such as, trust, love and compassion.

Defining Your Values

Now I want you to do one of the most important self-development exercises there is and define your values.

1. In your journal write down all the values that come to mind.

2. When you have written as many as you can take a look at your list. Add or cross off values until you feel you have your definitive top ten.

As a side note: There are no right or wrong answers when it comes to the values you choose. Allow yourself to be totally honest and think laterally.

Core Values

Now establish which of these ten values are your most important. Look at your list. Which five values are you willing to give up and which five can you not live without?

Cross out your values until you have your top five. Next, make sure they are in order of importance, so your number one value is at the top of the list and so on. Now take away the last two values on your list so you are left with your top three. Study these values for a moment. These little monkeys are the reasons why you have the life you do. Your top three values are your master, your judge and jury. Honoring them or not honoring them has created happiness or unhappiness in your life. Make sure that these three are indeed your main ones and that they are in the correct order of importance.

Honoring Your Values

To honor your values you have to live by them. That means before you make a decision, always consciously consider your values. Review your values on a regular basis as they can change over time without you being aware of it.

Conflict Of Interest

There are times when two or more of your top values may come into conflict. When this happens, situations will arise to test your top value. For example, let's say your top value is 'loyalty,' and your second is 'integrity.' Imagine a situation that temporarily has you abandoning loyalty over integrity. Perhaps you do value integrity over loyalty most of the time, but still live as if loyalty is number one. Another scenario would be if your top value of unconditional love came up against honesty. How would you react? Is being honest better than loving unconditionally?

It is not always simple to honor all of your top values at once. Your authentic top value will usually win through. Certain situations can test your value system so when they do, honor your top values as best you can. They make great learning experiences that nearly always result in increased self-awareness and self-confidence.

Real-Life Story

I had been coaching Angela for about six months when she came to me with a particular issue just before Halloween. She told me about her brother, Steven, who even at 28 years old, (several years younger than her), was still her a 'kid' brother. Angela explained that she loved her brother dearly and wanted him to be happy. He'd had several serious relationships which all ended in tears, so she was delighted when he was enthusiastic about his new girlfriend Sarah. So much so she became a regular at family parties. Angela got to know her quite well but felt she wasn't right for her brother. Even though he seemed really taken with her, there was something about Sarah Angela didn't trust.

Angela's hunch was soon proven to be correct. Steven had made a frantic phone call to Angela at 2.00 a.m. He had just found out Sarah was seeing someone else. Angela tried to calm Steven as they had heart to heart. During this conversation, Angela found out many things about Sarah. This information confirmed to her that Sarah wasn't a very nice person after all. Steven claimed that Sarah's infidelity was the last straw. He never wanted to see her again. Angela confessed she was a little relieved about his decision.

Angela soon forgot all about the situation until Thanksgiving. She arrived at her parent's house only to see Sarah sitting and happily chatting away to Steven. It turned out to be a bad Thanksgiving for Angela. The day had been ruined because she was mad at Steven for taking Sarah back. She was also mad at her parents for welcoming her into their home. Of course she was particularly mad at Sarah for treating her brother so badly in the first place.

Needless to say Angela ate and left as quickly as possible. The next day she called her Mom to tell her how she felt. Angela asked her mother why she thought it was ok to have Sarah in the house after all she had done to Steven. Her mother had explained that she didn't want to make things difficult for Steven or alienate him from family parties because of Sarah's behavior. Angela argued that by doing this she was encouraging the relationship that would ultimately leave her brother heartbroken again. Angela announced that she wouldn't play a part in it. She gave her mother an ultimatum. If Sarah was invited for Christmas, then she would not come.

The Coach Approach

When Angela had finished telling me this story I asked her how she felt. She said she felt bad because of how this had split the family in two. But she was not going to back down on how she felt. I asked Angela to remind herself of her top three values.

She told me they were unconditional love, honesty and compassion. I suggested that she had a possible conflict between her two most important values. Angela realized what she had been doing. Her value of honesty was overriding her top value of unconditional love. In other words, Angela's strong belief in being honest about her brother's relationship was coming before her unconditional love for her brother. This conflict was ruining her relationship with him and making her miserable. We discussed that her demand for everyone to be honest was putting a condition on her love for her brother and family.

The Result

Angela learned that her unconditional love for her brother was indeed her top value. She honored it by keeping her feelings about Sarah to herself. Angela and her family enjoyed a wonderful Christmas which indeed included Sarah. Steven is now engaged to Sarah and its ok with Angela. But she did ask me if I could coach him out of it!

How To Make Your Wishes Come True

'If you play it safe in life you've decided that you don't want to grow anymore.'
Shirley Hufstedler

Stage Four gave you the opportunity to think of your most outrageous dream. Now I am going to take you through a goal setting system that will bring your wishes to life. This is one of the longest exercises in the book. It will work best if you take the time to complete it all in one go.

Take one item from the wish list you made earlier. Ask yourself the following:

- How long have I wanted this to happen?

- How would achieving it change my life?

- If this is something that I have wanted for a long time, why don't I have it yet?

For the last question write a list of your reasons. It could be because of your parents, spouse, employer or colleague. Or perhaps it's because of the economy or a fear that you have.

The truth is, all the above are just excuses. They are the kind of things we blame when we don't get what we wish for. Why is it hard to get what we want? What is the secret? Is it luck? Actually, getting what you want is up to you. The power lies within your mind. This is the good news. The not-so-good news is this power is in your *subconscious* mind. That is the challenge. How do you access or control such a thing?

The reason we struggle to get what we want is because our subconscious can sabotage our efforts. A perfect example of this is when we want to lose weight. We may start dieting but after several days we give into temptation. It seems we want one thing but do another. Now we have an inner-conflict. Consciously we want to lose weight, but subconsciously we don't want to deprive ourselves of our favorite foods.

Here's more good news. You are not doomed to suffer these conflicts forever. Your subconscious can be controlled. You can make it work with you instead of against you.

What I am about to teach you is different to any other goal setting system you have tried before. It's the only one that makes both your conscious and subconscious work in total harmony.

Answer this:

How interested are you in learning more about this goal setting system? Think of a number between 1 and 10 where 10 means 'very interested' and 1 means 'not at all interested.'

What I just did was ask you to use your internal rating system. This is because it uses your instinct instead of your intellect. If you did select a number between one and ten, you made a judgment based on your inner-feelings rather than your intellect. You had little information about the goal system so you couldn't use your intellect, instead you had to use your intuition for judging your interest. It is important to tune into this powerful resource. It improves your internal communication and is especially helpful in situations when you don't have all the facts. Use it to guide you as often as possible. Its main benefit though, is that it brings your subconscious into line with what you truly desire.

Go back to all the wishes you have written down during this book. Rate them using these criteria;

1. Desirability
2. Difficulty

Using your intuition, take your wishes and rate them out of ten for desirability. Ten means totally desirable and one means not very desirable. Next, rate their difficulty factor. How easy are they to achieve? Ten means very difficult and one means easy.

This rating system is why you don't always achieve what you want. If you discover a wish isn't as desirable as you first thought, you will not be driven to achieve it. Similarly, if it appears too difficult, you will end up abandoning it.

Take a look at your wishes. How difficult and desirable are they? If you have given any of your wishes low scores take them off your list. You have just proven that they are not good enough for you.

For this exercise, concentrate on one of your wishes that has a score of seven or above in both categories. Write a detailed description of your wish. To help you do this, answer the following:

- What are your feelings about your wish?

- What is the best scenario that comes to mind?

- What other imagery comes to mind when you think about it?

- What ideas spring to mind?

- What colors, smells, sounds and tastes appear?

Bring as much life as possible to your wish using your imagination. Take time to re-check it for desirability and difficulty. The next important element is to see if you have any hidden reservations about making it happen. Doing this will counter-act your subconscious minds' sabotaging power.

Think about whether your wish comes into conflict with any of your values. If so, re-think and re-write it until all your doubts have gone. Also, ensure that achieving your wish only relies on *your* actions and not anyone else's. Your wishes should always depend on you alone. They should also be flexible enough to endure the unpredictable like weather conditions, any form of cancellation or equipment and technological failure.

Think about when you want your wish to happen. Give yourself an end date. Write it down. For example:

'By July 8th 2009, I will have/do/be....'

Giving your wish a deadline will make it feel more real and obtainable. Now your wish is not an *if* it's a *when*. You can get excited about the approaching date and use the time in between to prepare. Ensure that your deadline is realistic. Wishes should be challenging, not impossible. But don't make the date too far ahead either because then you will find it hard to stay motivated.

Now you have a clear description of your wish along with the perfect closing date. All you need now is an action plan. Take your date and work out in stages how to achieve your goal. Then, in regular and appropriate intervals, work backwards starting from today right up to your deadline. Note in detail what you have to do first then next and so on to make your wish come true. Put them into organized stages.

By using this system you dissolve any overwhelming tasks and turn them into achievable steps to move you towards your goal. For example, if your wish is to run a marathon then you need to start training at least eighteen weeks before. Each stage of your training builds up gradually so the whole experience becomes an enjoyable challenge.

Be as detailed and as accurate as possible with your descriptions of each stage. Regularly check to see if you are on track. Be realistic and don't forget to incorporate some fun along the way.

Here is just a simple example of how to break down your planning into stages within a timeline. I use months, but it could easily be days, weeks or even years. Note where each stage should end and fill in what you have to do within each stage before you can move onto the next.

	Stage One	Stage Two	Stage Three	Stage Four
March	Start			
April				
May				
June	Finish	Start		
July				
August		Finish	Start	
September				
October			Finish	Start
November				
December				End Date!

Now I am going to give you a little success insurance. At the end of your wish description, write the following:

'Please make this, or something better, happen in ways that are for the highest good for me and everyone else.'

This very simple line is quite effective. It helps to plant your wish favorably within your subconscious. Also, it takes care of any negative feelings you may still have about getting what you want. In essence it encourages you to believe that something better than what you have described could actually happen.

Heads Up!

You may develop signs of inner-conflict during your journey towards achieving your wish. This is where your improved self-awareness skills can help. You need to pick up on any signs of conflict quickly in order to prevent them from sabotaging your plans. Signs include feeling apathetic or guilty. Watch out for these as they can be very subtle and even disguised. For example, let's say your goal is to run a marathon but one day you feel too tired to train. Tiredness is a sign of inner-conflict. When this happens, simply acknowledge it. It is probably your ego trying to put you off so don't give in to it.

Similarly, be aware of signs that your efforts are working. Look for signs that you are moving in the right direction. Signs include when things start to become easier and more exciting. This is your inner-self signaling that all is well. You are in the flow and your subconscious is in harmony with your goal. If, however, you don't have these feelings of excitement then you may be encountering some kind of block, so look into it. If you don't manage to reach your goal it will be because of one of these two reasons: either you didn't plan properly or because you were not fully in tune with your internal feedback signals.

If you have followed these instructions you now have at least one wish that is achievable, yet challenging. It's very desirable and honors your values. Ideally, all your doubts towards achieving it have been eliminated, and you have a timeline with regular action points to keep you on track.

Building Upon Your Success

Create momentum with your wishes. Take time to celebrate each achievement and then dive straight into another one. This ensures that the energy and good feelings you have about your achievement feeds into your next one. You may juggle several at once. It will be easier to do this if each one has a different deadline. Attempt ones that have variable difficulty levels too because if you experience success relatively quickly, it will give you the confidence to attempt a more ambitious one next.

How To Use Your Body To Create Happiness

Believe it or not, your body and how you use it is fundamental to your happiness. This section is about how you *use* your body. Your physicality directly influences your happiness. Becoming more aware and proactive about how you move can help you create feelings of happiness very easily. To prove this, I want you to stand up. This works best if you are alone, you will see why in a moment! Stand as straight as you can with your shoulders back, your chin up and smile as hard as you can. Now try and feel sad about something.

It's hard isn't it? When your body is positioned in such a way, it's almost impossible to feel down. If you did manage to think about something sad, did you notice if your posture changed at all?

Now try the reverse. Sit or stand slumped over. Your chin is on your chest and you are staring at the floor with the corners of your mouth turned down. Frown. Now think of something exciting. Again, it's difficult to do so because your body is expressing an opposing mood.

The lesson here is that if you want to change your mood, change your posture. The effect is instant. You can go from feeling and looking sad, to bright and cheerful just by a swift change in your stance and facial expression. Practice it. See how it works for you. Get familiar with how you hold yourself when you are in a certain mood. To help you do this, think of something that really excites you and gets you whipped up into a frenzy. Concentrate on it for a few minutes then take a note of the following:

- What is your posture like?
- Where are your hands?
- How are your feet positioned?
- How fast are you breathing?
- How do you feel inside?
- How warm does your body feel?
- What expression do you have on your face?
- Are you moving around or standing still?
- If you are moving, how quickly?

Notice how your thoughts or mood affect your physicality in this particular state. Do the same with other states too. Note the details and then try to switch your mood just by using your body. Practicing and perfecting this gives you the power to change your mood whenever you feel like it. You have probably used this technique before without realizing it. For example, at work you may have needed to have felt more alert and so sat bolt upright with your head held high.

This exercise does not work as effectively with deep states of depression. This is because depression harbors more complex emotions and require specialized attention. However, you can use this exercise to give yourself more personal power when you need it.

How To Eliminate Problems

As women we tend to ruminate on our problems and connect them back to some unchangeable aspect of ourselves. So I thought it might be helpful to give you some advice on how to overcome any issue that you may find along your journey.

First, you have to understand that there will always be some kind of challenge to face in life. No one has a problem-free existence. This is a good thing. Without challenges you wouldn't grow. As I mentioned before, some choose to ignore their problems in the hope that they will go away. When faced with a problem you must take action. Every action you take will be rewarded with important information about what works for you. If you don't, then you will never learn anything new. Even if the action you take doesn't work, at least you will have learned that so you can try something else.

Tackling an issue is easier if you break it down. This immediately takes the enormity out of it. Start by looking at which part of the issue you can do something about immediately. Then look at what you can resolve shortly after that. Soon you will be creating a solid solution.

Think of a challenge you are facing right now. Break it down and answer the following:

- How am I responsible for this?

- What can I learn from this situation?

- What are the top three options for resolving it?

- Which one will produce the best outcome?

- What is the very first step I should take?

Once you have arrived at a first step you are on your way to solving the problem. When you have resolved it, reflect upon what you learned.

Be philosophical about the obstacles you face. This will free up your creativity when it comes to developing an appropriate and positive solution.

In life, you will never be given a problem that is too much for you. That would be pointless. No matter how big the issue is, look for the first step to take. See how quickly you gain control over it. See the big picture and the opportunities within it.

Review of Stage Six

I could say you are an incredible person for getting to this stage, but you already know this by now! You have achieved a great deal in this stage so congratulate yourself.

Now you are moving towards a happier life at great speed with great goals and your top three values intact. You are fast approaching the final stage of this system. But before you continue, just ponder the following:

1.   What has changed for you since starting Stage Six?

2.   Have any of your perceptions changed?

3.   What are your top three values?

4.   How do you honor these every day?

5.   What are your top three wishes?

6.   How confident are you that you can achieve them?

7.   What challenge in your life can you start working on today?

Stage Seven

How To Live Happily Ever After

'Nothing seems beyond my reach. I know that, with courage, I can follow my heart no matter what.' **Marcy Basel**

In this seventh and final stage you will learn the following:

- The importance of self-care
- How consistency is key
- How to create a life mission and vision
- How to live your dream life
- How to ask for and receive help
- How to create your legacy
- How to harness your brainpower
- How to live happily ever after

Throughout our childhood we love to be told stories set in magical far off lands. These tales would spark off our imagination as we dreamt of the big adventures we would have when we were grown ups. As an adult you may have been able to relive these adventures through your children's bedtime stories. But have you ever wondered how many of us actually live the dreams we imagined so many years ago? Ok, so your dream life may be slightly different to what it was back when you were ten, but are you any closer to living it? If not, this stage will help. Answer the following:

- What was your childhood dream?
- How is it different today?
- Are you living your dream in any way? If so, how?
- If not, why not?

I always encourage people to dream and dream big! I want them to revisit their imagination and creativity. You are once again allowed to dream. So I want you to dream big and believe that living your dream is possible. This time your dream gets to be your reality. Re-think the value of dreaming because it's good for you and essential to your short and long-term happiness.

In this final part I have split the book into two main topics. The first part concentrates on making the most out of your life now. The second is even more exciting and life-changing as you create your dream life and your legacy. We will do this by taking a mental time machine into your future and beyond your lifetime. This stage is all about being happy now and in the future so get ready to learn some new tricks that even Harry Potter would be proud of!

A philosophy of mine is that happiness thrives when you are in harmony with yourself and the world around you. The previous stages have, at the very least, helped you to become more self-aware. Now you are ready to intensify the relationship you have with yourself. It's time to take a big bite out of life and create a new lifestyle based around your happiness. Here's the really good news. You already have everything you need to do this. It's just a case of putting everything you have learned into action. This seventh and final stage will help you do just that.

The Importance Of Self-Care

Your health is one of the most important aspects of your life. If you do not have your health it is harder to be happy. You have to get fit and stay fit. The question is how can you do that without boring yourself to death with endless dieting and exercise programmes? The truth is few of us mere mortals actually like exercising. It can be a tedious process and one that has given birth to a million and one excuses for not doing it. Here's the thing. I know that getting and staying highly motivated about fitness is challenging. Any enthusiasm we manage to gather together can quickly wear off and we are left staring at a new and expensive piece of exercise equipment collecting dust in the basement.

I think we need to get real about fitness. In order for us to be able to get fit and stay fit for the rest of our lives, we need to find something we actually like doing. I favor this technique over doing what those countless and hour-long exercise infomercials suggest. Besides, starting and stopping fitness regimes is exhausting emotionally, physically and often financially too.

What fitness regime is right for you? What do you like to do? Walk? Go for bike rides? Play tennis? Dance? Swim? You can get fit many different ways. You just need to do whatever it is you like to do often enough. It's true that our fast-paced world is tiring enough. Chasing around after a family is a daily workout in itself. The difference is that by doing something you really like, you are doing something for yourself that builds up your strength, energy and staying power.

Think of the benefits. You can actually enjoy your exercise time. Until now, you have probably never regarded exercise as a treat. The effort, sweat, grueling nature and monotony dominates our perception of it. But doing it this way means you can treat yourself as often as you want to! If you re-think fitness as 'a personal timeout' instead of a time for working out, then it can become a whole new experience.

With any exercise it's always best to start small and gradually build up. For example, walking just a little further and at a quicker pace each day can make all the difference. Get up and move around as much as you can at home or at work. Stretch like a cat as often as public decency allows. You do not have to change everything you do overnight, instead slowly introduce a little more here and there. Avoid great fanfares, announcements and news releases of your intentions. Just do it quietly. This way you avoid other people's opinions! Think about how you can add more activity each week. Eventually, you will have an active, enjoyable and regular regime that feels good. Then you have cracked the code to physical fitness. This is something that millions of women have never been able to do and suffer as a result.

If you are already disciplined at keeping fit then ensure you have a balanced regime and take time to relax too. The golden rule for keeping fit is to eat less and exercise more. This is all you have to know. If you follow this rule for the rest of your life, you will never have to worry about your weight or fitness levels again.

Eat Right
Dieting must be one of the most boring things ever. Diet fad after diet fad keeps us obsessed with finding the secret to losing weight. The truth is all we really have to do is maintain a balance. Remember the old phrase: 'everything in moderation?' It's as true today as it has always been. Nowadays we use the word 'balance' instead.

Our wellbeing needs harmony in all areas of our life. This is especially important when it comes to food. Substitute unhealthy food with a healthier alternative. It's easy! For example, substitute mashed potatoes with boiled or baked. Sugary cereals can be replaced with healthier ones and add your own fruit for sweetness. Also, change the way you cook. Grill instead of fry. When you eat out, do not go for a creamy pasta dish. Ask for your pizza with no cheese. Being inventive and creative means you never have to diet.

Never deprive yourself and also never overindulge beyond the usual holiday feasts. Look to find a happy medium, a balance that suits you. Feel good about yourself every time you eat.

Look at what you buy every week and check that you are getting the best quality foods you can afford. Check for freshness and avoid foods with added salt or sugar.

Calorie counting is also a boring obsession. Refrain from being fixated about calories. Eating should be a pleasant experience not a time to feel guilty or punish yourself. Having negative associations with food causes us to start and stop diets frequently. Yo-yo dieting is very unhealthy for you. Unless you are on a special medical diet, all you have to do is eat healthy, fresh food regularly.

Planning your meals in advance does help. This way you can ensure you incorporate a good balance of different foods throughout the week.

Ask yourself:

- Which food can I live without?

- Which food have I always wanted to try?

- How can I make my meals more exciting and healthful?

Having kids to feed can usually disrupt the best thought out eating plan. However, you are the head of the household and know best when it comes to your family's health, so take charge. If you face too much of a rebellion, then plan your meals separately. But don't be tempted by left-over peanut butter sandwiches! Snacking between meals is a big temptation. Reach for fruit instead.

I am no dietician or nutritional expert. I am only making informed suggestions that are in line with my own philosophy about wellbeing which is to love what you do, love what you eat and love who you are. If all these are in harmony, and we don't blame our hormones for our habits, then we can forget the stranglehold and misery that dieting has had over us and just enjoy food.

The Biggest Temptation

Chocolate! I love it! Much has been written about it recently and now we know it's good for us. Great! Of course it has to be good quality chocolate. I go for any brand that contains at least 70% cocoa. Enjoy it, but don't over do it.

Positive Pampering

Have you noticed how some people are always immaculately groomed? Maybe you are one of them. For some, taking care to look their best makes them feel good. Positive pampering is about taking good care of yourself. By pampering I mean taking the time to have your nails, hair and feet done or to have facials and massages. It's about enjoying being a woman. It is not about vanity or outer-beauty. It's more to do with honoring your femininity. Unfortunately, surprisingly few women pamper themselves as much as they should. Usually it's only before a vacation or a big event like a wedding that some ever get to visit a spa. Don't let a lack of time, money or feelings of guilt prevent you from being pampered regularly. It doesn't have to be expensive or take all day. Think about how you would like to add a little more pampering time into your calendar.

Your Happy Hour

Start dedicating at least one hour a week to your wellbeing. Be it pampering, exercising or just sitting and reading your favorite book or magazine. This is *your* time. Ensure you have no interruptions or distractions. Savor this time with yourself. Get to know yourself a little more. Re-introduce into your life the things you love. Read the books, play the games, walk in the places and try the exercises that you haven't had time to before. Make the most of it and do it regularly.

By taking time to give back to your wellbeing, you are honoring yourself and your physical and mental worth. If you have any negative feelings about pampering yourself try and eliminate them now. Don't let them stop you.

If you already have a good regime in place, take time to help a friend.

How Consistency Is Key

An additional key to achieving health and happiness is consistency. This means being consistent with your values, beliefs, regimes, thoughts and goals. It is the magic ingredient for making amazing progress. It is also the foundation from which you grow an improved, happier life. Being consistent means you are fixed, firm, determined and driven, but not necessarily stubborn or inflexible. It gives you inner-strength. Furthermore, it's an admirable quality to have and one that commands respect.

Now you have learned more about yourself and what you want out of life, you need to use consistency to bring everything to fruition. Being consistent is a habit that replaces many others. It's a habit of action. It ensures you do what you need to do to get where you want to go.

Take a look back to a time when you were consistent and answer the following:

- What did you achieve during that time?

- What made you act consistently?

Next answer the following:

1. Are you consistent, consistently?
2. If not, why not?
3. How do you perceive consistency?
4. Do you have any negative thoughts about being consistent?

5. If so, why?
6. What would happen if you became more consistent in just one area of your life?
7. What improvements could you make today to ensure you remain consistent with your goals and desires?

Having A Bad Day?

When talking about creating a dream life, the last thing you'd expect to discuss is perspective. Well you are right. On this occasion, I am not talking about putting your life into perspective, but your *results* into perspective.

It is important not to judge yourself too harshly when you are trying to improve your life. When you are busy pushing forward and making great progress, you can sometimes push yourself too far. This will make you feel exhausted and disillusioned. Know that it's ok to have a bad day. Having a day when you are not thinking about happiness or have made a mistake is perfectly acceptable. Put it into perspective. You are just having one of *those* days. Life doesn't always make sense so don't worry about it. Shrug it off and move on. Dwelling on your errors or worrying about why you are not feeling dynamic and super-happy will only deprive you of energy. The important thing is how you react to a bad day and what you do to console yourself.

Never take drastic action after one or two bad days. Just start fresh with a clear mind the following day. If you have several weeks of 'bad days' you should review your goals to see if they are in line with your values or are achievable for you at this time. See if there is anything missing from your intentions that would help you to re-energize and get back on track.

Predetermining what might set you back is a good strategy that can serve you well. Thinking ahead of yourself and predicting what or who may cause disruptions to your plans can make all the difference to your level of success.

Go back to your wish list. Review them and write what possible obstacles your may encounter when you try to make them come true. Take into account people, your environment, finances, family, yourself and anything else you can think of. Next, take each potential obstacle in turn and see how you can avoid it. But above all, always look for the opportunity when you are having a bad day.

How To Create A Life Mission & Vision

This next section looks at two of the most important elements for living happily ever after. Take out your journal and get ready to create your future by devising your own life mission and vision.

Life Mission

Creating a mission statement is not just for the corporate world. Mission statements help a corporation create their ideal direction. If that sounds good to you, why not create one for yourself? Finding your mission in life is above and beyond the goals you have set so far. Uncovering your mission is to discover your reason for being here on Earth. It may be one of the most important actions you will ever take.

What Is A Mission Statement?

Your mission statement is a declaration of your life's purpose. It is a summary of your primary goals and dreams. It will act as a guide for any decisions that you make. Without a mission statement you have little direction. Don't be one of those people who never plan further than a few years ahead, if at all. Create your own life-purpose statement. Having one will accelerate you forward both personally and professionally because it helps you to define your calling, your true purpose in life.

All the great leaders of this world have a clear sense of their mission in life. It is what they think about most of the time. All their decisions are based around their mission. If any action can move them closer to achieving it, they take it. Think of some of the world's great leaders and other successful people throughout time. What do you think their missions were?

Your Mission
It's time for you to join the elite and successful both past and present. Get your journal and get ready to give yourself a truly amazing gift, a life with a defined mission. Your mission statement has to be specific, so writing 'I will be happy' is not enough. You need to work the magic. Write a mission statement that is no longer than one sentence and is simple enough for an eight year old to understand. Think about what you would really like to achieve. What would make you happy?

Example of a mission statement:

'My aim in life is to help women achieve their dream of having a happier and more fulfilling life.'

Your statement should be simplistic, direct, clear and easy to remember. Making a complicated statement will only serve to confuse and frustrate you. You have to be clear about what you intend to do. This makes it easier for you to define the tasks necessary to fulfill it. Play around with your statement until it says what it needs to say in the clearest way possible. Get to know it by heart. Then write down the tasks necessary to achieving your mission in a logical sequence. See how they correlate with your other goals. Do they differ at all? How are they similar? Make suitable adjustments to your goals so that each one is in line with your mission statement. Check the following:

- Do all your goals help you achieve your mission?

- Will any of them hinder your progress?

Get busy fine tuning your mission statement because the next topic will be taking it a stage further. Get prepared for what comes next by having a clear and concise mission statement with a logical progression of goals and deadlines.

Extra Info: Review your mission statement regularly to ensure that it is always relevant and achievable. Make sure you always have an up-to-date statement to refer to. Remember this, you either have a mission statement of your own, or you live by someone else's. Which would you prefer?

Life Vision

While a mission statement is all about what you want to do in your life, your life's vision is the personal outcome of completing it. A life vision is about looking into the future. It's creating an ideal image for yourself and using it to guide and inspire you. Having such a vision feeds your soul. It gives you a great lust for life and motivates you towards creating an exciting and irresistible future.

A big part of creating happiness is in believing your future is going to be extraordinary. Define your vision. Leave nothing out except limitations.

Your vision is the big picture, the color and the light, while your goals are the building blocks you use to create it. Now that you have goals and a mission, you can create your life vision. Creating a vision only requires a little imagination and the belief that there are no limits. Think big because it creates a more compelling vision. The more riveting the image you have, the more you will want to achieve it. Add as much detail as possible to your vision so it is clear, vibrant and easy to replicate.

Are you ready? Still have your journal near by? Good. You need to visualize your future first then write it down. Remember, think big!

Part One:
Write down your life's vision by imagining what a day living it would be like. Imagine you have traveled twenty years into your future. Think about the following:

- Where are you?
- What are you doing?
- What are you wearing?
- What do you look like?
- Who is with you?
- What do you see, hear, smell and feel?

Write down your answers in the present tense as if it is happening now. Feel the excitement of living this life as if you have already achieved it.

Part Two:
Hold that image in your mind and start adding more detail to it: Describe things in detail, like your home, family and environment. Take everything into account, professionally, personally and spiritually.

- What are you doing on a day-to-day basis?

- Who is living with you?

- Who is working with you?

- How much are you worth financially?

- How do you feel?

Now you have an animated, full color living picture of a typical day in your future. This image can grow depending on how much thought you give it. It is your perfect excuse to start daydreaming so you can build a vivid picture in your mind which is full of detail. This image should become familiar to you. For this to happen re-live the vision again and again adding more to it each time. Once it becomes engrained into your mind, you will believe that it will come true. After all seeing is believing.

Once you have a clear vision and have expressed this vision as something that you want, your subconscious will start to find ways to make it happen. Write your vision down in detail. Cut out pictures from magazines to help illustrate it. Give yourself something to aim for that is truly desirable. When you cultivate a desire in a precise way you will start to notice opportunities that can help you take steps towards achieving it.

How To Live Your Dream

Living your vision, your dream life, should score ten out of ten on the happiness scale. Make sure you keep your vision and goals with you so you can read them and develop them as often as possible. They should become a main guide for you in life along with your mission statement. Work steadily through your life vision goals and see how the momentum of achieving one makes such an enormous difference to your life. You will start to truly grow and develop as an individual and move yourself along on your journey successfully.

Scoring a twelve out of ten on the happiness scale, however, is where extreme dreaming comes into play. Think about your vision for a moment. Now think about adding to it to make it even more dynamic. Ask yourself:

• What would I have to add or take away from my vision to make it the best ever?

- Am I thinking big enough?
- Do I have a negative belief or limiting thought affecting my vision?

This is your invitation to go wild with your vision. After all, it's yours and no one else's. If you only have one life, don't you want to make it the best possible?

A word of warning: don't let friends, family or loved ones put you off creating your dream. They may have a completely different mindset to the one you have developed. This is also a very personal exercise, so your idea of a dream life might not be theirs. It is a great exercise for couples to do though. If you have a partner, create your visions separately and then compare notes to see how alike they are. Of course, you may have to make adjustments to make sure you fit everything in to please you both.

Good luck with your scoring and make sure you keep adding to your vision until you can add no more. Set yourself a high standard to aim for and have fun with it.

How To Ask For & Receive Help

Being proactive about creating happiness is one way to get it. However, you may need a little assistance along the way. As I have mentioned earlier, some people are a little uncomfortable asking for, or receiving help. Unfortunately, this can only prevent them from getting what they truly deserve. There is nothing quite as sad as getting so far in life only to give up right at the last minute because what came next could not be achieved alone. Goals that rely on other people to succeed are no good, but that doesn't mean to say you won't need a little help along the way. There is no shame in asking for help. Doing so shows courage and intelligence. Not asking for help is to risk never seeing your vision turn into a reality. No one can be successful all by themselves. All those who achieve great things never do so alone. Look at how many people are involved in writing a book, making a movie, a TV show or organizing an event. It is the same for you and your life. If you see gaps in how to get from A to B, then ask for guidance from someone who has already succeeded in that area.

Remember, you do not have to follow their advice, but it may inspire you to take another form of action. Approach others for assistance and they will be flattered that you asked them and will be more than happy to help. Open up your heart and mind to receive what you desire and ask for help if you need it. Have you ever heard the phrase 'ask and you shall receive?' It's true, so start asking and enjoy receiving.

How To Create Your Legacy

Leaving behind a legacy, something of great worth and value to the world is always admired. Have you ever thought about leaving the world a good example of how to live an extraordinary and successful life?

Think about all the people alive today who are living a successful, creative and productive life. If they could do it then you can too! What makes you less able? Is it a lack of time, money or ability? I believe the only difference is that they *decided* to do something extraordinary and carried it out. Once they had made such a decision their intention alone would have propelled them forward.

Often, a legacy is bigger than the individual who creates it. It demands that you think beyond your own needs and devote your efforts to the needs of others. There are no sacrifices, only dedication. The reward is that what you create will help change people's lives for the better and for long after you have gone. There is a legacy hiding in each and every one of us. What's yours? What gift do you have for the world?

Being aware of what your unique gift is gives you a complete understanding of how you fit into the world. This next exercise requires your concentration, imagination, creativity and spirit. All of which you have in abundance. What you are about to do is visualize your legacy in as much detail as possible. Read through the exercise first before you attempt it. First of all, free your imagination from any self-imposed limitations. Sit somewhere where you won't be disturbed. Close your eyes and start to imagine in your mind's eye your own funeral. Don't worry, for this exercise we assume you have lived a long and very successful life. But we need to go forward enough in time so you can look back and see the life you created for yourself.

Imagine that you are looking down on the occasion. You can see and hear everything very clearly. Take a good look around. Notice the following:

- Which friends, colleagues, associates and partners fill the room?
- Which family members are there?
- Who else is there?

Next, imagine three individuals standing up to read a eulogy. The first one is read by a family member. They talk about what kind of person you were. He or she describes your personality, your home life and what it was like being related to you.

The second person is somebody famous, anybody you choose. They talk about what you contributed to the world. They describe how you helped and influenced others and made a real difference. Finally, they describe how your legacy is to continue on without you.

The third and final speech is from a friend. They talk about how you helped them personally and the difference you made to their life and what it meant to them.

Each tribute describes your legacy from different perspectives. Now it is up to your imagination to add the detail. Don't think of this exercise as morbid. Rather, it is a celebration of who you were and what you achieved.

One of my all time favorite questions is:

'If you knew you could not fail, what would you do?'

When I first heard this question it changed my life forever. It opened up the whole world for me. Ask yourself that question. In this book you have hopefully learned that there is no such thing as failure. We only make mistakes. If you know you cannot fail, what do you want to do? What do you feel needs to be said, done or changed in the world?

Legacy building is taking your life to a different level and never looking back. It's about embracing the future with an open heart and mind. Now you know what you know, is there any way that you cannot create a legacy of your own?

Start now! Take what you have gleaned from your visualization and write it down alongside your life vision. Consider the following:

- How do they work together?
- What additions can you make to them so they are in complete harmony?
- What are the first steps you need to take and when?
- What step would follow that?
- Then what step would follow that?

Break your legacy down in to bite-size pieces. Make it easy to see each step. Then, follow through. Before you know it, you will have made a great deal of progress. Don't forget you have the universe on your side. Asking for help, guidance and wisdom when you need it will ensure your success.

How To Harness Your Brainpower

We have more brainpower than we realize. Our brains have the answer to any question we ask it. It is the most extraordinary organ we possess. Although men may beg to differ! But they would probably agree that the brain is something we have yet to fully comprehend and utilize. I have learnt that we can live happier and more fulfilling lives simply by adjusting the way we utilize our brainpower. Think about it for a moment. Whenever you ask yourself a question your brain always supplies an answer. That is how your brain works. If it does not supply an answer immediately, just wait a while. It will get back to you eventually.

There is one issue though. The answers our brain's supply may not always be what we had hoped for. In fact, the answers may well be hurtful. For example, if you ask your brain, 'why does this always happen to me?' It may well answer, 'because you are foolish and trust people too much!' Hmmm, not exactly constructive!

Well, here's the trick. It is not the brain's answer that is the issue; it is your question that could do with some adjustment. You see, your brain provides an answer that directly mirrors the quality of the question it was asked. As we all know, if you ask a stupid question, you get a stupid answer. The same is true when we ask ourselves a question. If you ask your brain an intelligent question, you will receive an intelligent answer. Now you own a resource that knows no boundaries and is yours to use whenever you need it. Try it out. Ask yourself a poor quality question and see what comes back to you. Next, think of an issue you have. Ask your brain an intelligent question about it. Here's a tip: a good quality question is usually one that is proactive and searching, rather than complaining or negative.

For example, start your questions with: 'How can I...?' Or 'In what way can I....?' One example is: 'How can I make this year the very best?' Starting a question like this is asking your brain to come up with real solutions. Your brain never lets you down as long as you ask it properly. Many of the questions I have asked you in this book have been designed to get the best quality answers from you. Go back and look at how they are structured so you can follow the same format.

How To Live Happily Ever After

Every year most of us sit down with family and friends to give thanks. Some of us do this once or twice a week in our place of worship. Also, at certain times we give our loved ones gifts. The biggest secret to living happily ever after is to enhance both your giving and thanks so that they become the center of everything you do. There is nothing like being thankful and having the ability to give. They are two of life's greatest rewards.

Thanks

Above and beyond what you do with your family or community, develop a strong feeling of gratitude for everything that comes your way. Be thankful for the good times and the not-so-good times. They all will have added something positive to your life. Give thanks for all the people who have come into your life including those who have hurt you. They too will have taught you a valuable lesson about yourself. Every night take some time out to express your thanks to the world. Be thankful for what you have had, what you have now and what is yet to come.

This attitude towards life conquers destructive emotions like anxiety, hatred, jealousy, unworthiness and loss. It also helps us keep a clear perspective on how far we have come in life. Be extra thankful, even in testing times. When you don't feel particularly fortunate, give thanks anyway. It will change your outlook and mood helping you make the most out of a poor situation.

Giving

We all know the power of giving. My school motto was, 'in giving we receive' and nothing is as true. How wonderful to be in a world where you get rewarded for the actions you take. Each action has an impact on our lives and the lives of others. So give without thinking of the reward and watch how your good deeds will come back to you tenfold. Not only does the thought of helping others make us feel good, it raises our self-esteem. Try and think what you can give in any situation instead of thinking 'what's in it for me?' Watch how your world changes for the better.

Only give what you can. Being a martyr goes against the belief that this is an abundant world. There is nothing intelligent or good about making yourself suffer or creating more poverty by giving everything away. Giving has to be a win-win situation. Give what you can and do it often. You can give money, gifts, your time, your expertise or just your presence. Learn to be appreciated and learn how good it feels to have the power to help people.

Take out your journal and write down ways that you can become an extraordinary giver. You can give to your family, your neighborhood or even globally:

- How can you help others consistently?
- What do you have that you can readily give?

Think about your life now and see how you can make extra time for giving or volunteering for a good cause. Make time for it and see how quickly you are rewarded. Put into action a plan for giving for the rest of your life so your existence has positively affected as many people as possible. By helping others you are helping yourself and by giving to others you are rewarding yourself. This is the basis of living happily ever after.

The Healing Power Of Laughter

Finally, how often do you throw your head back and laugh until your eyes water and your mascara runs down your cheeks? Laughing has amazing feel good powers and we should try and do it more often. It's good for us and it feels great.

Laughing at our situation, especially one we feel is incomprehensible helps us to approach it more energetically. Let go of trying to figure out why life plays the way it does and remember your sense of humor. Don't take things too seriously or make situations more dramatic than they actually are. In every situation look for the humour and ask yourself what can you do to laugh more often?

Review of Stage Seven

My heart and love go out to you for completing The Happiness System. I hope you have enjoyed the journey. There was so much to think about, what with building legacies and all! But I thought answering a few questions would help you seal what you have learned:

- How have you changed your routine to incorporate more time for yourself?
- Look back at your mission statement, how has creating it changed the way you think about your life?
- What is your favorite part of your life vision and why?
- At which point along the way do you anticipate some help?
- What can you do today to prepare for that moment?
- How does your legacy define who you are?
- How different are you from the person who started reading this book?
- What is the most exciting thing you have planned to do because of this book?
- What was the most important lesson you learned from this book?
- Is there any part of this book you feel unsure about or need to review?
- On a scale of 1 to 10, how determined are you to have the happiest and most fulfilling life possible?

You are an extraordinary human being for coming this far and by actively looking to improve your life. You should have learned quite a lot about yourself and the world in general. Maybe you adopted a new perspective on life too? Go back to Stage Three and review your Happiness Quotient, how do you score now?

You now have the tools and know-how to create the most exquisite life for yourself and your family. Regularly refer back to the work you have completed to keep all your plans alive. Keep a daily journal from now on and record your thoughts and ideas. Monitor your progress whilst planning your future in greater detail. The extraordinary part of self-development is being able to look back to see how far you have come. Having a sense of purpose and improved self-knowledge makes you happier. You feel more alive and more connected with everyone and everything

Be determined to have the life you desire and deserve. Know your potential and believe you can do it. Fulfill your potential. Don't let anything or anybody prevent you from growing and becoming the person you were meant to be. Come back to this system at anytime. Whenever you feel you need support and encouragement, you will find it in these pages. Keep learning and keep growing all your life.

Remember to live with your S.E.L.F

Self-awareness
Empathy
Love
Forgiveness

Resources:

Below is information on where to find a coach or how to become a Professional Life Coach:

International Coach Federation
1444 "I" Street NW Suite 700
Washington, DC 20005
Phone: 888-423-3131
202-712-9039
Fax: 888-329-2423, 202-216-9646
Email: icfoffice@coachfederation.org
URL: www.coachfederation.org

Coach University
PO Box 512, Andover, KS, 67002, USA
Toll Free Phone: 1-800-48COACH (1-800-482-6224)
Toll Free Fax: 1-800-FAX5655 (1-800-329-5655)
Phone: 1-719-227-1333 (for callers outside of North America)
Fax: 1-316-733-1760
Email: admissions@coachinc.com
URL: www.coachu.com

The Coaches Training Institute
1879 Second Street
San Rafael, CA 94901
415-451-6000
Call Toll Free: 1-800-691-6008
Fax: 415-460-6878 Email: info@thecoaches.com

Recommended Reads:
These are just some of the amazing book out there that can help you continue on your life improvement journey.

Marcus Aurelius, Meditations
Martha Beck, Finding Your Own North Star
The Bible
The Bhagavad-Gita
Boethius, The Consolation Philosophy
Deepak Chopra, The Seven Spiritual Laws Of Success
Deepak Chopra, Ageless Body, Timeless Mind
Wayne W Dyer, Meditations For Manifesting
Jack Kornfield, Mediation For Beginners
Paulo Coelho, The Alchemist
Stephen Covey, The 7 Habits Of Highly Effective People
Stephen Covey, The 8th Habit
The Dhammapada
Ralph Waldo Emerson, Self Reliance
Louise Hay, You Can Heal Your Life
Susan Jeffers, Feel The Fear And Do It Anyway
Lao Tzu, Tao Te Ching
Norman Vincent Peale, The Power Of Positive Thinking
Marianne Williamson, A Return To Love
Iyanla Vanzant, In The Meantime
Don Miguel Ruiz, The Mastery Of Love
Brain Klemmer, If How To Books Were Enough
Cynthia Kersey, Unstoppable
Napoleon Hill, Think and Grow Rich
Eckhart Tolle, The Power Of Now
M Scott Peck, The Road Less Traveled
John Gray, How To Get What You Want & Want What You Have
Mark Victor Hansen & Jack Canfield, Chicken Soup For The Soul series
Robert Allen & Mark Victor Hansen, The One Minute Millionaire

About The Author

Alexandra Watson is The Happiness Coach for Women. She has helped countless women create happy and fulfilling lives with her know-how, warmth, encouragement and support. She has worked with Fortune 500 companies, educational conferences and many professional associations for over fifteen years. Also, Alexandra regularly has articles on women's happiness issues published internationally. Alexandra is married and hoping to start a family soon.

Alexandra is a member of the following: Life Coaching Academy, International Coach Federation (ICF), International Association of Coaches (IAC) and Coachville.

Alexandra is the co-founder of the **Women's Life Improvement Club**. It is the premiere provider of first-class life improvement programs and events for women who are ready to enhance and re-energize their lives. Subscribe to her free monthly newsletter and if you want to discover the best kept secret to life improvement go to **www.WliClub.com**

A Request From Alexandra

I always want to hear your success stories and any feedback you may have about my book. If you would like to share with others how it helped you improve your life please email me directly at HappinessAuthor@aol.com.

If you are interested in other books from my series, or audio programs, workbooks or my up and coming seminars, please go to my website for more details: **www.AlexandraWatson.com**.

Thank you!

Printed in the United Kingdom
by Lightning Source UK Ltd.
107689UKS00001B/253-273